THE BHAGAVAD GĪTĀ

THE BHAGAVAD GĪTĀ

TRANSLATED AND INTERPRETED BY
FRANKLIN EDGERTON

HARVARD UNIVERSITY PRESS
CAMBRIDGE, MASSACHUSETTS
1972

This book was originally published as Volumes 38 and 39 of the Harvard Oriental Series. It is here reprinted in one volume. The Sanskrit text and Sir Edwin Arnold's translation have been omitted in this edition, and revisions have been made in the Preface and the Notes to the Translation.

Printed in the United States of America

To the memory of Maurice Bloomfield

CONTENTS

PREFACE

THIS book is the precipitate of many years of occupation with "India's favorite Bible," as I called the Bhagavad Gītā in my little "interpretation" of 1925. It still seems a good name for it. For, to quote the same source, "it has permeated the collective religious consciousness of the people, from one end of India to the other," so that "not to know it means among them almost what it would mean for an English-speaking person not to know the Bible." It is a prime source of inspiration for many of the political and intellectual leaders of the Indian people, typified by Mahatma Gandhi, who was even more a cultural nationalist than a political one. Becoming known in Europe and America little more than a century ago, it quickly won the interest and admiration of such leaders of thought as Von Humboldt in Germany and Emerson in America. Some philosophical and religious groups in this country today regard the Gītā almost as highly as the Hindus do.

There is a widening circle of intelligent westerners who are losing their occidental insularity and coming to realize that India, like some other eastern countries (China, for instance), has created great works of civilization, of arts and letters and thought, in practically every field of human culture. Any educated man and woman must know at least that such things exist; that civilization does not stop at Suez; that there is a great Indian literature—art—philosophy—music, and so on. And some are learning that it is really not hard to get directly acquainted with some of the more accessible products of Indian literature and art; and that the experience is enjoyable and profitable.

I am firmly convinced that no one can know—in any worth-while sense—any of India's cultural products without learning some Sanskrit. But that is not so serious a hurdle as is often supposed. Even if one lacks the linguist's interest in language as such (and to the linguist Sanskrit is, for various reasons, one of the most interesting of languages), anyone who has a reasonable knack for languages can learn in one year to read the simpler styles of Sanskrit literature with appreciation and enjoyment, though not without some help from a dictionary.

I trust that my book will help those who may want to use the Gītā as an aid to fluency in the Sanskrit language and an introduction to Hindu religion at the same time. The first part contains the translation. While the translation is fairly literal, I hope it is not un-English, nor yet wholly unfaithful to the style and spirit of the original. No attempt has been made to keep to verbal identity between this translation and the English versions of stanzas or passages in my "interpretation" in the second part, which are freer, though the general sense is, of course, always the same. Occasional uncertainties or difficulties of interpretation are treated in the Notes to the Translation, which are placed at its end. In them I have recorded interpretative differences of opinion, which seemed to me important, from some of my predecessors, particularly the two most celebrated Hindu commentators, Saṃkara and Rāmānuja, and six of the leading modern translators: the Hindu Telang, the Germans Garbe and Deussen, the Frenchman Senart, and the Britons Barnett and Hill (see my Notes on Bibliography and Exegesis, below).

The second part contains a careful revision of my "interpretation," mentioned above (*The Bhagavad Gītā or Song of the Blessed One,* Chicago, Open Court, 1925). Some errors have been eliminated, and a somewhat different turn has been given to the treatment of some subjects, notably in the introductory chapters. In general, however, my views have not materially changed; my account of the main thread of the Gītā's thought and of its historic setting remains essentially the same.

There are many commentaries, translations, and interpretations of the Gītā other than those listed. So many, indeed, that some may ask, why publish another? One partial justification may be found in the pedagogical aims of this book, mentioned above. But I shall not deny that I hope scholars and advanced students will also find it useful.

For, paradoxical as it may appear, despite the seeming simplicity of most of the Gītā's language, there are many details that have been differently interpreted. And less surprising, perhaps, is the fact that general estimates of its fundamental philosophy have varied widely, from the times of the ancient Hindu commentators to the present day. Like many another religious book, it is taken to prove almost anything. Perhaps there will be something subjective, inevitably, in any interpretation of such a work. Perhaps any one reads into it something of himself. I can only say, on this point, that I have tried my best to be objective: to present what the author seems to have meant, whether I liked it or not.

I do not know how many times I have read the entire Gītā; thirty or forty times at least. More important is the fact that I have worked over most of it minutely with students (any teacher knows what that means) at least fifteen to twenty times, trying to extract the meaning of every particle. The result contains not a little that differs from any previous interpretation, in small things and great. I am not so presumptuous as to claim finality for any of it. But I feel that I have now reached the saturation point, as far as this text is concerned. It is unlikely that "this person" can ever progress much farther towards the understanding of it. Let this stand, then, simply as a record of the best that *one* western Sanskritist could do with the Gītā, after half a lifetime of the most earnest effort. If it is still very imperfect, that fact in itself will be significant. And even in that case, a few things here and there may commend themselves to posterity, and so contribute to the ultimate goal, the final interpretation which will doubtless never be written.

NOTES ON THE BIBLIOGRAPHY AND EXEGESIS OF THE GĪTĀ

THE bibliography of the Gītā in modern times is almost endless. It has been translated into probably all important modern languages, and into some of them many times. I shall mention here only six translations — three English, two German, and one French — which seem to me important from the scholarly standpoint, and which I have constantly consulted in my interpretation of the text. The translation of Arnold belongs in quite a different category; it has no value for scholars as such. The six translations are:

K. T. Telang, *The Bhagavadgītā*. Sacred Books of the East, Vol. 8. Oxford, 1882; 2d ed. 1908. References here are to the first edition.
Richard Garbe, *Die Bhagavadgītā*. Leipzig, 1905; 2d ed. 1921. References are to the first edition.
L. D. Barnett, *The Bhagavadgītā*. London, 1905.
Paul Deussen, "in Gemeinschaft mit Dr. Otto Strauss," *Vier philosophische Texte des Mahābhāratam*. Leipzig, 1906.
Émile Senart, *La Bhagavadgītā*. Paris, 1922.
W. Douglas P. Hill, *The Bhagavadgītā*. Oxford and London, 1928.

Rarely are other translations or interpretations referred to in this work. But I have used extensively, especially on doubtful or disputed interpretations, the two best-known Hindu commentaries in Sanskrit: namely those by Śaṃkara (abbreviated Ś) and Rāmānuja (R). While they have the defects of all ancient Hindu commentators, they still have considerable value for the judicious student. For both I have used the excellent editions in the Ānandāśrama Sanskrit Series.

Garbe's book contains not only a careful and excellent scholarly translation, but an introduction in which the translator undertakes an analysis and interpretation of the text which is profoundly different from mine, and which I criticized in the Appendix to my interpretation of 1925. According to Garbe, the text is a composite work. He believed that the original kernel was a "Sāṃkhya" treatise (using the term Sāṃkhya as denoting a dualistic philosophical system like that known in later India under this name), which was later worked over and expanded by an adherent of the (later) Vedānta philosophy. He thought he could detect and eliminate these later Vedānta accretions; and he printed them in a type of smaller size in his translation. His theory is now generally abandoned; I doubt if any one now holds to it,[1]

[1] The late Professor Winternitz, who was the greatest authority on the history of Indian literature, was one of those who once accepted Garbe's theory; but later, in the

and I shall not burden this book with a repetition of the arguments against it. It should, however, be emphasized that Garbe's theory of the composition of the poem does not detract at all from the value of his penetrating philological interpretation of the individual stanzas.

My own interpretation tacitly assumes the unity of the Gītā. There seems to me to be no definite reason for any other assumption. It is certain, at any rate, that for many centuries the Gītā has been handed down as a unit, in practically the form in which it now exists. The sanctity which it acquired in the eyes of the Hindus has protected it to an extraordinary degree from changes and from textual corruptions. Important variant readings in the very numerous manuscripts of the vulgate version are virtually non-existent,[2] and no far-reaching divergences occur in them.

In the Appendix to my former book (p. 99) I stated that "there is absolutely no documentary evidence that any other form of the Gītā than that which we have was ever known in India." This statement was true at the time, but must now undergo a slight modification. Since it was written, Professor F. Otto Schrader has discovered a Kashmirian version of the Gītā, which can be traced for nearly a thousand years, and which shows a rather considerable number of minor divergences from the vulgate text, and a very few additions and omissions of entire stanzas. (See his monograph, *The Kashmir Recension of the Bhagavadgītā*, Stuttgart, 1930.) In Professor Schrader's opinion, some of these differences are important; he thinks that in some cases they are older and more original than the readings of the vulgate. In this I differ with him, for reasons which I have set forth in my review of his work, *JAOS*. 52.68–75. I believe that the variant readings of the Kashmirian text are without exception late and secondary, and have no bearing on the determination of the oldest form of the Gītā. Even if I were wrong, however, the question would have little importance for the present work; for the differences are relatively very slight, and rarely affect the essential meaning of even single stanzas, never of the work as a whole.

I would not, however, be understood as asserting that there are no interpolations or secondary accretions in the Gītā. Before it acquired its present odor of sanctity, which has kept it for so many centuries substantially free from changes, it must have lived thru a human, undeified period,

English version of his *History of Indian Literature* (Vol. 1, Calcutta, 1927, p. 436), he abandoned it, tho he still was more inclined to dissect the Gītā than I am. A pupil of Garbe's, the late Rudolf Otto, has more recently carried dissection of the Gītā to a far greater extreme. I consider his work negligible; see my review in *The Review of Religion* (New York), 4.447 ff. (May, 1940).

[2] I believe that this statement will remain essentially true even after the appearance of the first critical edition of Book Six of the Mahābhārata (which includes the Gītā), now being prepared by Professor S. K. Belvalkar for the Bhandarkar Oriental Research Institute of Poona.

so to speak; and it is entirely possible that during that period some additions may have been made to it, or other changes introduced. I suppose that every careful student of the Gītā is likely to develop suspicions about occasional verses or passages. But the grounds for such suspicions must, in the nature of things, be subjective and tenuous. In no case can they be regarded as approximating scientific demonstration. And, in particular, the fact that a given verse or passage is logically inconsistent with other passages in the Gītā constitutes, in my opinion, absolutely no reason for suspecting that it is unoriginal. If my book does not show that, it will have failed indeed.

THE BHAGAVAD GĪTĀ

TRANSLATION

THE BHAGAVAD GĪTĀ

Translation

CHAPTER I

Dhṛtarāṣṭra said:

1. In the Field of Right, the Kuru-field,
   Assembled ready to fight,
   My men and the sons of Pāṇḍu as well,
   What did they do, Saṃjaya?

Saṃjaya said:

2. Seeing however the host of the sons of Pāṇḍu
   Arrayed, Duryodhana then
   Approached the Teacher (Droṇa),
   And spoke a word, the prince:

3. Behold of Pāṇḍu's sons this
   Great host, O Teacher!
   Arrayed by Drupada's son,
   Thy skillful pupil.

4. Here are heroes, great archers,
   Like unto Bhīma and Arjuna in battle,
   Yuyudhāna, and Virāṭa,
   And Drupada of the great car;

5. Dhṛṣṭaketu, Cekitāna,
   And the heroic king of Benares,
   Purujit, and Kuntibhoja,
   And the Śibi-king, bull of men;

6. Yudhāmanyu the valorous,
   And Uttamaujas the heroic,
   The son of Subhadrā, and the sons of Draupadī,
   All, aye all, men of great cars.

7. But of our men, who are the most distinguished
   Learn from me, best of brahmans, —
   Who are the leaders of my host;
   To name them, I declare them to thee.

8. Thy good self, and Bhīṣma, and Karṇa,
And battle-winning Kṛpa,
Aśvatthāman, and Vikarṇa,
And the son of Somadatta too;

9. And many other heroes,
Giving up life for my sake;
With various weapons and arms,
All skilled in conflict.

10. (Altho) insufficient (in number) this our
Host is protected by (the wise) Bhīṣma;
On the other hand, (while) sufficient, this their
Host is protected by (the unskilled) Bhīma.[1]

11. And (so) in all movements,
Stationed in your several places,
Guard Bhīṣma above all,
Each and every one of you.

12. Producing joy in his heart,
The aged grandsire of the Kurus
Roared a lion's roar on high,
And blew his conch-shell, full of valor.

13. Then conch-shells and drums,
Kettle-drums, cymbals, and trumpets,
All at once were sounded;
The sound was tremendous.

14. Then on the white-horse-yoked
Mighty car standing,
Mādhava (Kṛṣṇa) and the son of Pāṇḍu (Arjuna)
Blew their wondrous conch-shells:

15. Hṛṣīkeśa (Kṛṣṇa) blew Pāñcajanya,
Dhanaṃjaya (Arjuna) blew Devadatta,
The great shell Pauṇḍra blew
Wolf-belly (Bhīma) of terrible deeds.

16. (The shell) Anantavijaya (blew) the king
Yudhiṣṭhira, Kuntī's son;
Nakula and Sahadeva
(Blew) Sughoṣa and Maṇipuṣpaka.

17. And the king of Benares, supreme archer,
    And Śikhaṇḍin, of the great car,
And Dhṛṣṭadyumna and Virāṭa,
    And the unconquered Sātyaki,

18. Drupada and the sons of Draupadī,
    All together, O king,
And the great-armed son of Subhadrā,
    Blew their conch-shells severally.

19. That sound Dhṛtarāṣṭra's men's
    Hearts did rend;
And both sky and earth
    It made to resound, swelling aloft.

20. Then seeing arrayed
    Dhṛtarāṣṭra's sons, the ape-bannered (Arjuna),
When the clash of arms had already begun,
    Lifted up his bow, the son of Pāṇḍu,

21. And to Hṛṣīkeśa then words
    Like these spoke, O king.
Between the two armies
    Halt my chariot, O unshaken one,

22. Until I espy these
    That are drawn up eager to fight,
(And see) with whom I must fight
    In this warlike enterprise.

23. I will see those who are going to fight,
    Who are here assembled,
For Dhṛtarāṣṭra's ill-minded son
    Eager to do service in battle.

24. Hṛṣīkeśa, thus addressed
    By Guḍākeśa, O son of Bharata,
Between the two armies
    Halted the excellent car,

25. In front of Bhīṣma and Droṇa
    And all the kings,
And said: Son of Pṛthā, behold these
    Assembled Kurus!

26. There the son of Pṛthā saw stationed
Fathers and grandsires,
Teachers, uncles, brothers,
Sons, grandsons, and comrades too,

27. Fathers-in-law and friends as well,
In both the two armies.
The son of Kuntī, seeing them,
All his kinsmen arrayed,

28. Filled with utmost compassion,
Despondent, spoke these words:
Seeing my own kinsfolk here, Kṛṣṇa,
That have drawn near eager to fight,

29. My limbs sink down,
And my mouth becomes parched,
And there is trembling in my body,
And my hair stands on end.

30. (The bow) Gāṇḍīva falls from my hand,
And my skin, too, is burning,
And I cannot stand still,
And my mind seems to wander.

31. And I see portents
That are adverse, Keśava;
And I foresee no welfare,
Having slain my kinsfolk in battle.

32. I wish no victory, Kṛṣṇa,
Nor kingdom nor joys;
Of what use to us were kingdom, Govinda,
Of what use enjoyments or life?

33. For whose sake we desire
Kingdom, enjoyments, and happiness,
They are drawn up here in battle,
Giving up life and wealth:

34. Teachers, fathers, sons,
Grandsires as well,
Uncles, fathers-in-law, grandsons,
Brothers-in-law, and (other) kinsfolk.

35. Them I do not wish to slay,
    Even tho they slay (me), O slayer of Madhu,
Even for three-world-rulership's
    Sake; how much less for the sake of the earth!

36. Having slain Dhṛtarāṣṭra's men, to us
    What joy would ensue, Janārdana?
Evil alone would light upon us,
    Did we slay these (our would-be) murderers.

37. Therefore we should not slay
    Dhṛtarāṣṭra's men, our own kinsfolk.
For how, having slain our kinsfolk,
    Could we be happy, Mādhava?

38. Even if they do not see,
    Because their intelligence is destroyed by greed,
The sin caused by destruction of family,
    And the crime involved in injury to a friend,

39. How should we not know enough
    To turn back from this wickedness,
The sin caused by destruction of family
    Perceiving, O Janārdana?

40. Upon the destruction of the family, perish
    The immemorial holy laws of the family;
When the laws have perished, the whole family
    Lawlessness overwhelms also.

41. Because of the prevalence of lawlessness, Kṛṣṇa,
    The women of the family are corrupted;
When the women are corrupted, O Vṛṣṇi-clansman,
    Mixture of caste ensues.

42. Mixture (of caste) leads to naught but hell
    For the destroyers of the family and for the family;
For their ancestors fall (to hell),
    Because the rites of (giving) food and water are interrupted.

43. By these sins of family-destroyers,
    (Sins) which produce caste-mixture,
The caste laws are destroyed,
    And the eternal family laws.

44. When the family laws are destroyed,
    Janārdana, then for men
Dwelling in hell certainly
    Ensues: so we have heard (from the Holy Word).

45. Ah woe! 'Twas a great wickedness
    That we had resolved to commit,
In that, thru greed for the joys of kingship,
    We undertook to slay our kinsfolk.

46. If me unresisting,
    Weaponless, with weapons in their hands
Dhṛtarāṣṭra's men should slay in battle,
    That would be a safer course for me.

47. Thus speaking Arjuna in the battle
    Sat down in the box of the car,
Letting fall his bow and arrows,
    His heart smitten with grief.

Here ends the First Chapter, called Discipline of Arjuna's Despondency.[2]

CHAPTER II

Saṃjaya said:

1. To him thus by compassion possessed,
   His eyes tear-filled, blurred,
Despondent, this word
   Spoke the Slayer of Madhu.

The Blessed One said:

2. Whence to thee this faintheartedness
   In peril has come,
Offensive to the noble, not leading to heaven,
   Inglorious, O Arjuna?

3. Yield not to unmanliness, son of Pṛthā;
   It is not meet for thee.
Petty weakness of heart
   Rejecting, arise, scorcher of the foe!

Arjuna said:

4. How shall I in battle against Bhīṣma,
   And Droṇa, O Slayer of Madhu,
Fight with arrows,
   Who are both worthy of reverence, Slayer of Enemies?

5. For not slaying my revered elders of great dignity
   'Twere better to eat alms-food, even, in this world;
But having slain my elders who seek their ends, right in this world
   I should eat food smeared with blood.[1]

6. And we know not which of the two were better for us,
   Whether we should conquer, or they should conquer us;
What very ones having slain we wish not to live,
   They are arrayed in front of us, Dhṛtarāṣṭra's men.

7. My very being afflicted with the taint of weak compassion,
   I ask Thee, my mind bewildered as to the right:
Which were better, that tell me definitely;
   I am Thy pupil, teach me that have come to Thee (for instruction).

8. For I see not what would dispel my
   Grief, the witherer of the senses,
If I attained on earth rivalless, prosperous
   Kingship, and even overlordship of the gods.

Saṃjaya said:

9. Thus speaking to Hṛṣīkeśa,
   Guḍākeśa the Slayer of the Foe
'I'll not fight!' to Govinda
   Said, and was silent.

10. To him spoke Hṛṣīkeśa,
   With a semblance of a smile, son of Bharata,
Betwixt the two armies
   As he was despondent, these words:

The Blessed One said:

11. Thou hast mourned those who should not be mourned,
   And (yet) thou speakest words about wisdom![2]
Dead and living men
   The (truly) learned do not mourn.

12. But not in any respect was I (ever) not,
   Nor thou, nor these kings;
And not at all shall we ever come not to be,
   All of us, henceforward.

13. As to the embodied (soul) in this body
   Come childhood, youth, old age,
So the coming to another body;
   The wise man is not confused herein.

14. But contacts with matter,[3] son of Kuntī,
   Cause cold and heat, pleasure and pain;
They come and go, and are impermanent;
   Put up with them, son of Bharata!

15. For whom these (contacts) do not cause to waver,
   The man, O bull of men,
To whom pain and pleasure are alike, the wise,[4]
   He is fit for immortality.

16. Of what is not, no coming to be occurs;
   No coming not to be occurs of what is;
But the dividing-line of both is seen,
   Of these two, by those who see the truth.

17. But know that that is indestructible,
   By which this all is pervaded;
Destruction of this imperishable one
   No one can cause.

18. These bodies come to an end,
 It is declared, of the eternal embodied (soul),
Which is indestructible and unfathomable.
 Therefore fight, son of Bharata!

19. Who believes him a slayer,
 And who thinks him slain,
Both these understand not:
 He slays not, is not slain.

20. He is not born, nor does he ever die;
 Nor, having come to be, will he ever more come not to be.[5]
Unborn, eternal, everlasting, this ancient one
 Is not slain when the body is slain.

21. Who knows as indestructible and eternal
 This unborn, imperishable one,
That man, son of Pṛthā, how
 Can he slay or cause to slay — whom?

22. As leaving aside worn-out garments
 A man takes other, new ones,
So leaving aside worn-out bodies
 To other, new ones goes the embodied (soul).

23. Swords cut him not,
 Fire burns him not,
Water wets him not,
 Wind dries him not.

24. Not to be cut is he, not to be burnt is he,
 Not to be wet nor yet dried;
Eternal, omnipresent, fixed,
 Immovable, everlasting is he.

25. Unmanifest he, unthinkable he,
 Unchangeable he is declared to be;
Therefore knowing him thus
 Thou shouldst not mourn him.

26. Moreover, even if constantly born
 Or constantly dying thou considerest him,
Even so, great-armed one, thou
 Shouldst not mourn him.

27. For to one that is born death is certain,
 And birth is certain for one that has died;
Therefore, the thing being unavoidable,
 Thou shouldst not mourn.

28. The beginnings of things are unmanifest,
 Manifest their middles, son of Bharata,
Unmanifest again their ends:
 Why mourn about this?

29. By a rare chance one may see him,
 And by a rare chance likewise may another declare him,
And by a rare chance may another hear (of) him;
 (But) even having heard (of) him, no one whatsoever knows him.

30. This embodied (soul) is eternally unslayable
 In the body of every one, son of Bharata;
Therefore all beings
 Thou shouldst not mourn.

31. Likewise having regard for thine own (caste) duty
 Thou shouldst not tremble;
For another, better thing than a fight required of duty
 Exists not for a warrior.

32. Presented by mere luck,
 An open door of heaven —
Happy the warriors, son of Pṛthā,
 That get such a fight!

33. Now, if thou this duty-required
 Conflict wilt not perform,
Then thine own duty and glory
 Abandoning, thou shalt get thee evil.

34. Disgrace, too, will creatures
 Speak of thee, without end;
And for one that has been esteemed, disgrace
 Is worse than death.

35. That thou hast abstained from battle thru fear
 The (warriors) of great chariots will think of thee;
And of whom thou wast highly regarded,
 Thou shalt come to be held lightly.

36. And many sayings that should not be said
    Thy ill-wishers will say of thee,
Speaking ill of thy capacity:
    What, pray, is more grievous than that?

37. Either slain thou shalt gain heaven,
    Or conquering thou shalt enjoy the earth.
Therefore arise, son of Kuntī,
    Unto battle, making a firm resolve.

38. Holding pleasure and pain alike,
    Gain and loss, victory and defeat,
Then gird thyself for battle:
    Thus thou shalt not get evil.

39. This has been declared to thee (that is found) in Reason-method,[6]
    This mental attitude: but hear this in Discipline-method,
Disciplined with which mental attitude, son of Pṛthā,
    Thou shalt get rid of the bondage of action.

40. In it there is no loss of a start once made,
    Nor does any reverse occur;
Even a little of this duty
    Saves from great danger.

41. The mental attitude whose nature is resolution
    Is but one in this world, son of Kuru;
For many-branched and endless
    Are the mental attitudes of the irresolute.

42. This flowery speech which
    Undiscerning men utter,
Who take delight in the words of the Veda,[7] son of Pṛthā,
    Saying that there is nothing else,

43. Whose nature is desire, who are intent on heaven,
    (The speech) which yields rebirth as the fruit of actions,[8]
Which is replete with various (ritual) acts
    Aiming at the goal of enjoyment and power, —

44. Of men devoted to enjoyment and power,
    Who are robbed of insight by that (speech),
A mental attitude resolute in nature
    Is not established in concentration.

45. The Vedas have the three Strands (of matter) as their scope;
 Be thou free from the three Strands, Arjuna,
Free from the pairs (of opposites), eternally fixed in goodness,[9]
 Free from acquisition and possession, self-possessed.

46. As much profit as there is in a water-tank
 When on all sides there is a flood of water,
No more is there in all the Vedas
 For a brahman who (truly) understands.

47. On action alone be thy interest,
 Never on its fruits;
Let not the fruits of action be thy motive,
 Nor be thy attachment to inaction.

48. Abiding in discipline perform actions,
 Abandoning attachment, Dhanaṃjaya,
Being indifferent to success or failure;
 Discipline is defined as indifference.

49. For action is far inferior
 To discipline of mental attitude, Dhanaṃjaya.
In the mental attitude seek thy (religious) refuge;
 Wretched are those whose motive is the fruit (of action).

50. The disciplined in mental attitude leaves behind in this world
 Both good and evil deeds.
Therefore discipline thyself unto discipline;
 Discipline in actions is weal.

51. For the disciplined in mental attitude, action-produced
 Fruit abandoning, the intelligent ones,
Freed from the bondage of rebirth,
 Go to the place that is free from illness.

52. When the jungle of delusion
 Thy mentality shall get across,
Then thou shalt come to aversion
 Towards what is to be heard and has been heard (in the Veda).

53. Averse to traditional lore ('heard' in the Veda)
 When shall stand motionless
Thy mentality, immovable in concentration,
 Then thou shalt attain discipline.

Arjuna said:

54. What is the description of the man of stabilized mentality,
That is fixed in concentration, Keśava?
How might the man of stabilized mentality speak,
How might he sit, how walk?

The Blessed One said:

55. When he abandons desires,
All that are in the mind, son of Pṛthā,
Finding contentment by himself in the self alone,
Then he is called of stabilized mentality.

56. When his mind is not perturbed in sorrows,
And he has lost desire for joys,
His longing, fear, and wrath departed,
He is called a stable-minded holy man.

57. Who has no desire towards any thing,
And getting this or that good or evil
Neither delights in it nor loathes it,
His mentality is stabilized.

58. And when he withdraws,
As a tortoise his limbs from all sides,
His senses from the objects of sense,
His mentality is stabilized.

59. The objects of sense turn away
From the embodied one that abstains from food,
Except flavor; [10] flavor also from him
Turns away when he has seen the highest.

60. For even of one who strives, son of Kuntī,
Of the man of discernment,
The impetuous senses
Carry away the mind by violence.

61. Them all restraining,
Let him sit disciplined, intent on Me;
For whose senses are under control,
His mentality is stabilized.

62. When a man meditates on the objects of sense,
Attachment to them is produced.
From attachment springs desire,
From desire wrath arises;

63\. From wrath comes infatuation,
From infatuation loss of memory;
From loss of memory, loss of mind;
From loss of mind he perishes.

64\. But with desire-and-loathing-severed
Senses acting on the objects of sense,
With (senses) self-controlled, he, governing his self,
Goes unto tranquillity.

65\. In tranquillity, of all griefs
Riddance is engendered for him;
For of the tranquil-minded quickly
The mentality becomes stable.

66\. The undisciplined has no (right) mentality,
And the undisciplined has no efficient-force; [11]
Who has no efficient-force has no peace;
For him that has no peace how can there be bliss?

67\. For the senses are roving,
And when the thought-organ is directed after them,
It carries away his mentality,
As wind a ship on the water.

68\. Therefore whosoever, great-armed one,
Has withdrawn on all sides
The senses from the objects of sense,
His mentality is stabilized.

69\. What is night for all beings,
Therein the man of restraint is awake;
Wherein (other) beings are awake,
That is night for the sage of vision.

70\. It is ever being filled, and (yet) its foundation [12] remains unmoved –
The sea: just as waters enter it,
Whom all desires enter in that same way
He attains peace; not the man who lusts after desires.

71\. Abandoning all desires, what
Man moves free from longing,
Without self-interest and egotism,
He goes to peace.

72. This is the fixation that is Brahmanic,[13] son of Pṛthā;
Having attained it he is not (again) confused.
Abiding in it even at the time of death,
He goes to Brahman-nirvāṇa.[14]

Here ends the Second Chapter, called Discipline of Reason-method.

CHAPTER III

Arjuna said:

1. If more important than action
   The mental attitude is held of Thee, Janārdana,
Then why to violent action
   Dost Thou enjoin me, Keśava?

2. With words that seem [1] confused
   Thou apparently bewilderest my intellect.
So tell me one thing definitely,
   Whereby I may attain welfare.

The Blessed One said:

3. In this world a two-fold basis (of religion)
   Has been declared by Me of old, blameless one:
By the discipline of knowledge of the followers of reason-method,[2]
   And by the discipline of action of the followers of discipline-method

4. Not by not starting actions
   Does a man attain actionlessness,
And not by renunciation alone
   Does he go to perfection.

5. For no one even for a moment
   Remains at all without performing actions;
For he is made to perform action willy-nilly,
   Every one is, by the Strands that spring from material nature.

6. Restraining the action-senses
   Who sits pondering with his thought-organ
On the objects of sense, with deluded soul,
   He is called a hypocrite.

7. But whoso the senses with the thought-organ
   Controlling, O Arjuna, undertakes
Discipline of action with the action-senses,
   Unattached (to the fruits of action), he is superior.

8. Perform thou action that is (religiously) required;
   For action is better than inaction.
And even the maintenance of the body for thee
   Can not succeed without action.

9. Except action for the purpose of worship,
 This world is bound by actions;
Action for that purpose, son of Kuntī,
 Perform thou, free from attachment (to its fruits).

10. After creating creatures along with (rites of) worship,
 Prajāpati (the Creator) said of old:
By this ye shall procreate yourselves —
 Let this be your Cow-of-Wishes.

11. With this prosper ye the gods,
 And let the gods prosper you;
(Thus) prospering one the other,
 Ye shall attain the highest welfare.

12. For desired enjoyments to you the gods
 Will give, prospered by worship;
Without giving to them, their gifts
 Whoso enjoys, is nothing but a thief.

13. Good men who eat the remnants of (food offered in) worship
 Are freed from all sins;
But those wicked men eat evil
 Who cook for their own selfish sakes.

14. Beings originate from food;
 From the rain-god food arises;
From worship comes the rain(-god);
 Worship originates in action.

15. Action arises from Brahman,[3] know;
 And Brahman springs from the Imperishable;
Therefore the universal Brahman
 Is eternally based on worship.

16. The wheel thus set in motion
 Who does not keep turning in this world,
Malignant,[4] delighting in the senses,
 He lives in vain, son of Pṛthā.

17. But who takes delight in the self alone,
 The man who finds contentment in the self,
And satisfaction only in the self,
 For him there is found (in effect) no action to perform.

18. He has no interest whatever in action done,
Nor any in action not done in this world,
Nor has he in reference to all beings
Any dependence of interest.

19. Therefore unattached ever
Perform action that must be done;
For performing action without attachment
Man attains the highest.

20. For only thru action, perfection
Attained Janaka and others.
Also for the mere control of the world
Having regard, thou shouldst act.

21. Whatsoever the noblest does,
Just that in every case other folk (do);
What he makes his standard,
That the world follows.

22. For Me, son of Pṛthā, there is nothing to be done
In the three worlds whatsoever,
Nothing unattained to be attained;
And yet I still continue in action.

23. For if I did not continue
At all in action, unwearied,
My path (would) follow
Men altogether, son of Pṛthā.

24. These folk would perish
If I did not perform action,
And I should be an agent of confusion;
I should destroy these creatures.

25. Fools, attached to action,
As they act, son of Bharata,
So the wise man should act (but) unattached,
Seeking to effect the control of the world.

26. Let him not cause confusion of mind
In ignorant folk who are attached to action;
He should let them enjoy all actions,
The wise man, (himself) acting disciplined.

27. Performed by material nature's
Strands are actions, altogether;
He whose soul is deluded by the I-faculty
Imagines 'I am the agent.'

28. But he who knows the truth, great-armed one,
About the separation (of the soul) from both the Strands and action,
'The Strands act upon the Strands' —
Knowing this, is not attached (to actions).

29. Deluded by the Strands of material nature,
Men are attached to the actions of the Strands.
These dull folk of imperfect knowledge
The man of perfect knowledge should not disturb.

30. On Me all actions
Casting,[5] with mind on the over-soul,
Being free from longing and from selfishness,
Fight, casting off thy fever.

31. Who this My doctrine constantly
Follow, such men,
Full of faith and not murmuring,
They too are freed from (the effect of) actions.

32. But those who, murmuring against it,
Do not follow My doctrine,
Them, deluded in all knowledge,
Know to be lost, the fools.

33. One acts in conformity with his own
Material nature, — even the wise man;
Beings follow (their own) nature;
What will restraint accomplish?

34. Of (every) sense, upon the objects of (that) sense
Longing and loathing are fixed;
One must not come under control of those two,
For they are his two enemies.

35. Better one's own duty, (tho) imperfect,
Than another's duty well performed;
Better death in (doing) one's own duty;
Another's duty brings danger.

Arjuna said:

36. Then by what impelled does this
Man commit sin,
Even against his will, Vṛṣṇi-clansman,
As if driven by force?

The Blessed One said:

37. It is desire, it is wrath,
Arising from the Strand of passion,
All-consuming, very sinful;
Know that this is the enemy here.

38. As fire is obscured by smoke,
And as a mirror by dirt,
As the embryo is covered by its membrane-envelope,
So this (universe[6]) is obscured thereby.

39. By this is obscured the knowledge
Of the knowing one, by this his eternal foe,
That has the form of desire, son of Kuntī,
And is an insatiable fire.

40. The senses, the thought-organ, the consciousness,
Are declared to be its basis;
With these it confuses
The embodied (soul), obscuring his knowledge.

41. Thou therefore, the senses first
Controlling, O bull of Bharatas,
Smite down this evil one,
That destroys theoretical and practical knowledge.[7]

42. The senses, they say, are high;
Higher than the senses is the thought-organ;
But higher than the thought-organ is the consciousness;
While higher than the consciousness is He (the soul).

43. Thus being conscious of that which is higher than consciousness,
Steadying the self by the self,
Smite the enemy, great-armed one,
That has the form of desire, and is hard to get at.

Here ends the Third Chapter, called Discipline of Action.

CHAPTER IV

The Blessed One said:

1. This discipline to Vivasvant
   I proclaimed; 'tis eternal;
   Vivasvant told it to Manu,
   Manu spake it to Ikṣvāku.

2. Thus received in line of succession,
   The royal seers knew it.
   In a long course of time in this world this
   Discipline became lost, scorcher of the foe.

3. This very same by Me to thee today,
   This ancient discipline, is proclaimed.
   Thou art My devotee and friend, that is why;
   For this is a supreme secret.

Arjuna said:

4. Later Thy birth,
   Earlier the birth of Vivasvant:
   How may I understand this,
   That Thou didst proclaim it in the beginning, as Thou sayest?

The Blessed One said:

5. For Me have passed many
   Births, and for thee, Arjuna;
   These I know all;
   Thou knowest not, scorcher of the foe.

6. Tho unborn, tho My self is eternal,
   Tho Lord of Beings,
   Resorting to My own material nature
   I come into being by My own mysterious power.

7. For whenever of the right
   A languishing appears, son of Bharata,
   A rising up of unright,
   Then I send Myself forth.

8. For protection of the good,
   And for destruction of evil-doers,
   To make a firm footing for the right,
   I come into being in age after age.

9. My wondrous birth and actions
   Whoso knows thus as they truly are,
On leaving the body, to rebirth
   He goes not; to Me he goes, Arjuna!

10. Rid of passion, fear, and wrath,
   Made of Me, taking refuge in Me,
Many by the austerity of knowledge
   Purified, have come to My estate.

11. In whatsoever way any come to Me,
   In that same way I grant them favor.
My path follow
   Men altogether, son of Pṛthā.

12. Desiring the success of (ritual) acts,
   They worship the (Vedic) deities in this world;
For quickly in the world of men
   Comes the success that springs from (ritual) acts.

13. The four-caste-system was created by Me
   With distinction of Strands and actions (appropriate to each);
Altho I am the doer of this,
   Know Me as one that eternally does no act.

14. Actions do not stain Me,
   (Because) I have no yearning for the fruit of actions.
Who comprehends Me thus
   Is not bound by actions.

15. Knowing this, action was done
   Also by the ancient seekers of salvation.
Therefore do thou simply do actions,
   As was done of old by the ancients.

16. What is action, what inaction?
   About this even sages are bewildered.
So I shall explain action to thee,
   Knowing which, thou shalt be freed from evil.

17. For one must understand the nature of action, on the one hand,
   And must understand the nature of mis-action,
And must understand the nature of inaction:
   Hard to penetrate is the course of action.

18. Who sees inaction in action,
And action in inaction,
He is enlightened among men;
He does all actions, disciplined.

19. All whose undertakings
Are free from desire and purpose,
His actions burnt up in the fire of knowledge,
Him the wise call the man of learning.

20. Abandoning attachment to the fruits of action,
Constantly content, independent,
Even when he sets out upon action,
He yet does (in effect) nothing whatsoever.

21. Free from wishes, with mind and soul restrained,
Abandoning all possessions,
Action with the body alone
Performing, he attains no guilt.

22. Content with getting what comes by chance,
Passed beyond the pairs (of opposites), free from jealousy,
Indifferent to success and failure,
Even acting, he is not bound.

23. Rid of attachment, freed,
His mind fixed in knowledge,
Doing acts for worship (only), his action
All melts away.

24. The (sacrificial) presentation is Brahman; Brahman is the oblation;
In the (sacrificial) fire of Brahman it is poured by Brahman;
Just to Brahman must he go,
Being concentrated upon the (sacrificial) action that is Brahman.

25. To naught but sacrifice to the deities some [1]
Disciplined men devote themselves.
In the (sacrificial) fire of Brahman, others [2] the sacrifice
Offer up by the sacrifice itself.

26. The senses, hearing and the rest, others [3]
Offer up in the fires of restraint;
The objects of sense, sound and the rest, others [4]
Offer up in the fires of the senses.

27. All actions of the senses
And actions of breath, others [5]
In the fire of the discipline of control of self
Offer up, when it has been kindled by knowledge.

28. Sacrificers with substance, sacrificers with austerities,
Sacrificers with discipline likewise are others,
And sacrificers with study of the Sacred Word and with knowledge,
Religious men, with strict vows.

29. In the nether life-breath the upper life-breath offer up
Others,[6] likewise the nether in the upper life-breath,
Checking the courses of the upper and nether life-breaths,
Intent upon restraint of breath.

30. Others [7] restrict their food and (so)
Offer up the life-breaths in the life-breaths.
All these know what sacrifice is,
And their sins are destroyed by sacrifice.

31. Those who eat the nectar of the leavings of the sacrifice
Go to the eternal Brahman.
Not (even) this world is for him who does not sacrifice;
How then the next, O best of Kurus?

32. Thus many kinds of sacrifice
Are spread out[8] in the face[9] of Brahman.
Know that they all spring from action!
Knowing this thou shalt be freed.

33. Better than sacrifice that consists of substance
Is the sacrifice of knowledge, scorcher of the foe.
All action without remainder, son of Pṛthā,
Is completely ended in knowledge.

34. Learn to know this by obeisance (to those who can teach it),
By questioning (them), by serving (them);
They will teach thee knowledge,
Those who have knowledge, who see the truth.

35. Knowing which, not again to bewilderment
In this manner shalt thou go, son of Pāṇḍu;
Whereby all beings without exception
Thou shalt see in thyself, and also in Me.

36. Even if thou art of sinners
The worst sinner of all,
Merely by the boat of knowledge all
(The 'sea' of) evil shalt thou cross over.

37. As firewood a kindled fire
Reduces to ashes, Arjuna,
The fire of knowledge all actions
Reduces to ashes even so.

38. For not like unto knowledge
Is any purifier found in this world.
This the man perfected in discipline himself
In time finds in himself.

39. The man of faith gets knowledge,
Intent solely upon it, restraining his senses.
Having got knowledge, to supreme peace
In no long time he goes.

40. The man unknowing and without faith,
His soul full of doubt, perishes.
Not is this world, nor the next,
Nor bliss, for him whose soul is full of doubt.

41. Him that has renounced actions in discipline,
That has cut off his doubt with knowledge,
The self-possessed, no actions
Bind, O Dhanaṃjaya.

42. Therefore this that springs from ignorance,
That lies in the heart, with the sword of knowledge thine own
Doubt cutting off, to discipline
Resort: arise, son of Bharata!

Here ends the Fourth Chapter, called Discipline of Knowledge.

CHAPTER V

Arjuna said:

1. Renuncіation of actions, Kṛṣṇa,
   And again discipline Thou approvest;
   Which one is the better of these two,
   That tell me definitely.

The Blessed One said:

2. Renunciation and discipline of action
   Both lead to supreme weal.
   But of these two, rather than renunciation of action,
   Discipline of action is superior.

3. He is to be recognized as (in effect) forever renouncing (action),
   Who neither loathes nor craves;
   For he that is free from the pairs (of opposites), great-armed one,
   Is easily freed from bondage (otherwise caused by actions).

4. Of reason-method [1] and discipline as separate, fools
   Speak, not the wise;
   Resorting to even one of them, completely
   Man wins the fruit of both.

5. What place is gained by the followers of reason-method,
   That is reached also by the followers of discipline(-method).
   That reason-method and discipline are one
   Who sees, he (truly) sees.

6. But renunciation, great-armed one,
   Is hard to attain without discipline;
   Disciplined in discipline, to Brahman the sage
   Goes in no long time.

7. Disciplined in discipline, with purified self,
   Self-subdued, with senses overcome,
   His self become (one with) the self of all beings,
   Even acting, he is not stained.

8. 'I am (in effect) doing nothing at all!' — so
   The disciplined man should think, knowing the truth,
   When he sees, hears, touches, smells,
   Eats, walks, sleeps, breathes,

9. Talks, evacuates, grasps,
Opens and shuts his eyes;
'The senses (only) on the objects of sense
Are operating' — holding fast to this thought.

10. Casting (all) actions upon Brahman,[2]
Whoso acts abandoning attachment,
Evil does not cleave to him,
As water (does not cleave) to a lotus-leaf.[3]

11. With the body, the thought-organ, the intelligence,
And also with the senses alone,
Disciplined men perform action,
Abandoning attachment, unto self-purification.

12. The disciplined man, abandoning the fruit of actions,
Attains abiding peace;
The undisciplined, by action due to desire,
Attached to the fruit (of action), is bound.

13. All actions with the thought-organ
Renouncing, he sits happily, in control,
The embodied (soul), in the citadel of nine gates,
Not in the least acting nor causing to act.

14. Neither agency nor actions
Of the (people of the) world does the Lord (soul) instigate,
Nor the conjunction of actions with their fruits;
But inherent nature operates (in all this).

15. He does not receive (the effect of) any one's sin,
Nor yet (of) good deeds, the Lord (soul);
Knowledge is obscured by ignorance;
By that creatures are deluded.

16. But if by knowledge that ignorance
Of men's souls is destroyed,
Their knowledge like the sun
Illumines that Highest.

17. Their consciousness and soul fixed on that (Highest),
With that as their final goal, supremely devoted to that,
They go to (the state whence there is) no more return,
Their sins destroyed by knowledge.

18. In a knowledge-and-cultivation-perfected
  Brahman, a cow, an elephant,
And in a mere dog, and an outcaste,
  The wise see the same thing.

19. Right in this world they have overcome birth,
  Whose mind is fixed in indifference;
For Brahman is flawless and indifferent;
  Therefore they are fixed in Brahman.

20. He will not rejoice on attaining the pleasant,
  Nor repine on attaining the unpleasant;
With stabilized mentality, unbewildered,
  Knowing Brahman, he is fixed in Brahman.

21. With self unattached to outside contacts,
  When he finds happiness in the self,
He, his self disciplined in Brahman-discipline,
  Attains imperishable bliss.

22. For the enjoyments that spring from (outside) contacts
  Are nothing but sources of misery;
They have beginning and end, son of Kuntī;
  The wise man takes no delight in them.

23. Who can control right in this life,
  Before being freed from the body,
The excitement that springs from desire and wrath,
  He is disciplined, he the happy man.

24. Who finds his happiness within, his joy within,
  And likewise his light only within,
That disciplined man to Brahman-nirvāṇa
  Goes, having become Brahman.

25. Brahman-nirvāṇa is won
  By the seers whose sins are destroyed,
Whose doubts are cleft, whose souls are controlled,
  Who delight in the welfare of all beings.

26. To those who have put off desire and wrath,
  Religious men whose minds are controlled,
Close at hand Brahman-nirvāṇa
  Comes, to knowers of the self.

27. Putting out outside contacts,
  And fixing the sight between the eye-brows,
Making even the upper and nether breaths,
  As they pass [4] thru the nose;

28. Controlling the senses, thought-organ, and intelligence,
  The sage bent on final release,
Whose desire, fear, and wrath are departed —
  Who is ever thus, is already released.

29. The Recipient of worship and austerities,
  The Great Lord of the whole world,
The Friend of all beings —
  Me knowing, he goes to peace.

Here ends the Fifth Chapter, called Discipline of Renunciation of Actions.

CHAPTER VI

The Blessed One said:

1. Not interested in the fruit of action,
   Who does action that is required (by religion),
He is the possessor of both renunciation and discipline (of action);
   Not he who builds no sacred fires and does no (ritual) acts.

2. What they call renunciation,
   Know that that is discipline (of action), son of Paṇḍu.
For not without renouncing purpose
   Does any one become possessed of discipline.

3. For the sage that desires to mount to discipline
   Action is called the means;
For the same man when he has mounted to discipline
   Quiescence is called the means.

4. For when not to the objects of sense
   Nor to actions is he attached,
Renouncing all purpose,
   Then he is said to have mounted to discipline.

5. One should lift up the self by the self,
   And should not let the self down;
For the self is the self's only friend,
   And the self is the self's only enemy.

6. The self is a friend to that self
   By which self the very self is subdued;
But to him that does not possess the self, in enmity
   Will abide his very self, like an enemy.

7. Of the self-subdued, pacified man,
   The supreme self remains concentrated (in absorption),
In cold and heat, pleasure and pain,
   Likewise in honor and disgrace.

8. His self satiated with theoretical and practical knowledge,[1]
   Immovable,[2] with subdued senses,
The possessor of discipline is called (truly) disciplined,
   To whom clods, stones, and gold are all one.

9. To friend, ally, foe, remote neutral,
   Holder of middle ground, object of enmity, and kinsman,
To good and evil men alike,
   Who has the same mental attitude, is superior.

10. Let the disciplined man ever discipline
   Himself, abiding in a secret place,
Solitary, restraining his thoughts and soul,
   Free from aspirations and without possessions.

11. In a clean place establishing
   A steady seat for himself,
That is neither too high nor too low,
   Covered with a cloth, a skin, and kuśa-grass,

12. There fixing the thought-organ on a single object,
   Restraining the activity of his mind and senses,
Sitting on the seat, let him practise
   Discipline unto self-purification.

13. Even[3] body, head, and neck
   Holding motionless, (keeping himself) steady,
Gazing at the tip of his own nose,
   And not looking in any direction,

14. With tranquil soul, rid of fear,
   Abiding in the vow of chastity,
Controlling the mind, his thoughts on Me,
   Let him sit disciplined, absorbed in Me.

15. Thus ever disciplining himself,
   The man of discipline, with controlled mind,
To peace that culminates in nirvāṇa,
   And rests in Me, attains.

16. But he who eats too much has no discipline,
   Nor he who eats not at all;
Neither he who is over-given to sleep,
   Nor yet he who is (ever) wakeful, Arjuna.

17. Who is disciplined (moderate) in food and recreation,
   And has disciplined activity in works,
And is disciplined in both sleep and wakefulness,
   To him belongs discipline that bans misery.

18. When the thought, controlled,
Settles on the self alone,
The man free from longing for all desires
Is then called disciplined.

19. As a lamp stationed in a windless place
Flickers not, this image is recorded
Of the disciplined man controlled in thought,
Practising discipline of the self.

20. When the thought comes to rest,
Checked by the practice of discipline,
And when, the self by the self
Contemplating, he finds satisfaction in the self;

21. That supernal bliss which
Is to be grasped by the consciousness and is beyond the senses,
When he knows this, and not in the least
Swerves from the truth, abiding fixed (in it);

22. And which having gained, other gain
He counts none higher than it;
In which established, by no misery,
However grievous, is he moved;

23. This (state), let him know, — from conjunction with misery
The disjunction, — is known as discipline;
With determination must be practised this
Discipline, with heart undismayed.

24. The desires that spring from purposes
Abandoning, all without remainder,
With the thought-organ alone the throng of senses
Restraining altogether,

25. Little by little let him come to rest
Thru the consciousness, held with firmness;
Keeping the thought-organ fixed in the self,
He should think on nothing at all.

26. Because of whatsoever thing [4] strays
The thought-organ, fickle and unstable,
From every such thing holding it back,
He shall bring it into control in the self alone.

27. For to him when his thought-organ is tranquil,
 To the disciplined one, supreme bliss
Approaches, his passion stilled,
 Become (one with) Brahman, stainless.

28. Thus ever disciplining himself,
 The disciplined man, free from stain,
Easily to contact with Brahman,[5]
 To endless bliss, attains.

29. Himself[6] as in all beings,
 And all beings in himself,
Sees he whose self is disciplined in discipline,
 Who sees the same in all things.

30. Who sees Me in all,
 And sees all in Me,
For him I am not lost,
 And he is not lost for Me.

31. Me as abiding in all beings whoso
 Reveres, adopting (the belief in) one-ness,
Tho abiding in any possible condition,
 That disciplined man abides in Me.

32. By comparison with himself, in all (beings)
 Whoso sees the same, Arjuna,
Whether it be pleasure or pain,[7]
 He is deemed the supreme disciplined man.

Arjuna said:

33. This discipline which by Thee has been explained
 As indifference,[8] Slayer of Madhu,
Thereof I do not see
 Any permanent establishment, because of (man's) fickleness.

34. For fickle is the thought-organ, Kṛṣṇa,
 Impetuous, mighty, and hard;
The restraining of it, I conceive,
 Is very difficult, as of the wind.

The Blessed One said:

35. Without doubt, great-armed one,
 The thought-organ is hard to control, and fickle;
But by practice, son of Kuntī,
 And by ascetic aversion, it may be controlled.

36. For one not self-controlled, discipline
    Is hard to reach, I believe;
But by the self-controlled man who strives
    It may be attained thru the proper method.

Arjuna said:

37. An unsuccessful striver who is endowed with faith,
    Whose mind falls away from discipline
Without attaining perfection of discipline,
    To what goal does he go, Kṛṣṇa?

38. Fallen from both, does he not
    Perish like a cloven cloud,
Having no (religious) foundation, great-armed one,
    Gone astray on Brahman's path?

39. This matter,[9] my doubt, O Kṛṣṇa,
    Be pleased to cleave without remainder;
Other than Thee, of this doubt
    No cleaver, surely, can be found.

The Blessed One said:

40. Son of Pṛthā, neither in this world nor in the next
    Does any destruction of him occur.
For no doer of the right
    Comes to a bad end, my friend.

41. Attaining the heavenly worlds of the doers of right,
    Dwelling there for endless years,
In the house of pure and illustrious folk
    One that has fallen from discipline is born.

42. Or else of possessors of discipline, rather,
    Enlightened folk, in their family he comes into existence;
For this is yet harder to attain,
    Such a birth as that in the world.

43. There that association of mentality
    He obtains, which was his in his former body;
And he strives from that point onward
    Unto perfection, son of Kuru.

44. For by that same former practice
    He is carried on even without his wish.
Even one who (merely) wishes to know discipline
    Transcends the word-Brahman (the Vedic religion).

45. But striving zealously,
With sins cleansed, the disciplined man,
Perfected thru many rebirths,
Then (finally) goes to the highest goal.

46. The man of discipline is higher than men of austerities,
Also than men of knowledge he is held to be higher;
And the man of discipline is higher than men of ritual action;
Therefore be a man of discipline, Arjuna.

47. Of all men of discipline, moreover,
With inner soul gone to Me
Whoso reveres Me with faith,
Him I hold the most disciplined.

Here ends the Sixth Chapter, called Discipline of Meditation.

CHAPTER VII

The Blessed One said:

1. With mind attached to Me, son of Pṛthā,
   Practising discipline with reliance on Me,
   Without doubt Me entirely
   How thou shalt know, that hear!

2. Theoretical knowledge to thee along with practical [1]
   I shall now expound completely;
   Having known which, in this world no other further
   Thing to be known is left.

3. Among thousands of men
   Perchance one strives for perfection;
   Even of those that strive and are perfected,
   Perchance one knows Me in very truth.

4. Earth, water, fire, wind,
   Ether, thought-organ, and consciousness,
   And I-faculty: thus My
   Nature is divided eight-fold.

5. This is My lower (nature). But other than this,
   My higher nature know:
   It is the Life (soul), great-armed one,
   By which this world is maintained.

6. Beings spring from it,[2]
   All of them, be assured.
   Of the whole world I am
   The origin and the dissolution too.

7. Than Me no other higher thing
   Whatsoever exists, Dhanaṃjaya;
   On Me all this (universe) is strung,
   Like heaps of pearls on a string.

8. I am taste in water, son of Kuntī,
   I am light in the moon and sun,
   The sacred syllable (*om*) in all the Vedas,
   Sound in ether, manliness in men.

9. Both the goodly odor in earth,
    And brilliance in fire am I,
  Life in all beings,
    And austerity in ascetics am I.

10. The seed of all beings am I,
    The eternal, be assured, son of Pṛthā;
  I am intelligence of the intelligent,
    Majesty of the majestic am I.

11. Might of the mighty am I, too,
    (Such as is) free from desire and passion;
  (So far as it is) not inconsistent with right, in creatures
    I am desire, O best of Bharatas.

12. Both whatsoever states are of (the Strand) goodness,
    And those of (the Strands) passion and darkness too,
  Know that they are from Me alone;
    But I am not in them; they are in Me.

13. By the three states (of being), composed of the Strands,
    These (just named), all this world,
  Deluded, does not recognize
    Me that am higher than they and eternal.

14. For this is My divine strand-composed
    Trick-of-illusion, hard to get past;
  Those who resort to Me alone
    Penetrate beyond this trick-of-illusion.

15. Not to Me do deluded evil-doers
    Resort, base men,
  Whom this illusion robs of knowledge,
    Who cleave to demoniac estate.

16. Fourfold are those that worship Me,
    (All) virtuous folk, Arjuna:
  The afflicted, the knowledge-seeker, he who seeks personal ends,[3]
    And the possessor of knowledge, bull of Bharatas.

17. Of these the possessor of knowledge, constantly disciplined,
    Of single devotion, is the best;
  For extremely dear to the possessor of knowledge
    Am I, and he is dear to Me.

18. All these are noble;
But the man of knowledge is My very self, so I hold.
For he with disciplined soul has resorted
To Me alone as the highest goal.

19. At the end of many births
The man of knowledge resorts to Me;
Who thinks 'Vāsudeva (Kṛṣṇa) is all,'
That noble soul is hard to find.

20. Deprived of knowledge by this or that desire,
Men resort to other deities,
Taking to this or that (religious) rule,
Constrained by their own nature.

21. Whatsoever (divine) form any devotee
With faith seeks to worship,
For every such (devotee), faith unswerving
I ordain that same to be.

22. He, disciplined with that faith,
Seeks to propitiate that (divine being),[4]
And obtains therefrom his desires,
Because I myself ordain them.

23. But finite fruition for them
That becomes, (since) they are of scant intelligence;
The worshipers of the gods go to the gods,
My devotees go to Me also.

24. Unmanifest, as having come into manifestation
Fools conceive Me,
Not knowing the higher essence
Of Me, which is imperishable, supreme.[5]

25. I am not revealed to every one,
Being veiled by My magic trick-of-illusion;
'Tis deluded and does not recognize
Me the unborn, imperishable, — this world.

26. I know those that are past,
And that are present, Arjuna,
And beings that are yet to be,
But no one knows Me.

27. It arises from desire and loathing,
 The delusion of the pairs (of opposites), son of Bharata;
Because of it all beings to confusion
 Are subject at their birth, scorcher of the foe.

28. But those whose sin is ended,
 Men of virtuous deeds,
Freed from the delusion of the pairs,
 Revere Me with firm resolve.

29. Unto freedom from old age and death
 Those who strive, relying on Me,
They know that Brahman entire,
 And the over-soul, and action altogether.[6]

30. Me together with the over-being and the over-divinity,
 And with the over-worship, whoso know,
And (who know) Me even at the hour of death,
 They (truly) know (Me), with disciplined hearts.

Here ends the Seventh Chapter, called Discipline of Theoretical and Practical Knowledge.

CHAPTER VIII

Arjuna said:

1. What is that Brahman, what the over-soul,
   What is action, O best of men,
   And what is called the over-being,
   What is said to be the over-divinity?

2. How and what is the over-worship here
   In this body, Slayer of Madhu?
   And how at the hour of death
   Art Thou to be known by men of self-control?

The Blessed One said:

3. Brahman is the supreme imperishable;
   The over-soul is called innate nature; [1]
   That which causes the origin of states of beings,
   The creative force, is known as action.[2]

4. The over-being is the perishable condition (of being),[3]
   And the spirit [4] is the over-divinity;
   The over-worship am I myself,[5] here
   In the body, O best of embodied ones.

5. And at the hour of death, on Me alone
   Meditating, leaving the body
   Whoso dies, to My estate he
   Goes; there is no doubt of that.

6. Whatsoever state (of being) meditating upon
   He leaves the body at death,
   To just that he goes, son of Kuntī,
   Always, being made to be in the condition of that.

7. Therefore at all times
   Think on Me, and fight;
   With thought-organ and consciousness fixed on Me
   Thou shalt go just to Me without a doubt.

8. If disciplined in the discipline of practice
   Be one's mind, straying to no other object,
   To the supreme divine Spirit
   He goes, son of Pṛthā, meditating thereon.

9. The ancient seer, the governor,
Finer than an atom — who meditates on Him,
The establisher of all, of unthinkable form,
Sun-colored, beyond darkness,

10. At the time of death with unswerving thought,
Disciplined with devotion and the power of discipline,
Making the breath to enter altogether between the eye-brows,
He goes to that supreme divine Spirit.

11. Which Veda-knowers call the imperishable,
Which ascetics free from passion enter,
Seeking which men live the life of chastity,
That place I shall declare to thee in brief.

12. Restraining all the gates (of the body),
And confining the thought-organ in the heart,
Fixing his own breath in his head,
Resorting to fixation of discipline,

13. The single-syllable Brahman (which is) *om*
Pronouncing, and meditating on Me,
Who departs, leaving the body,
He goes to the highest goal.

14. With thoughts ever straying to no other object,
Who thinks on Me constantly,
For him I am easy to gain, son of Pṛthā,
For the ever-disciplined possessor of discipline.

15. Having come to Me, rebirth,
Which is the home of misery and impermanent,
Do not attain the great-souled men
That have gone to supreme perfection.

16. As far as the world of (the personal god) Brahman, the worlds
Are subject to recurring existences, Arjuna;
But having come to Me, son of Kuntī,
No rebirth is found.

17. As compassing a thousand world-ages
When they know the day of Brahman,
And the night (of Brahman) as compassing a thousand ages,
Those folk know what day and night are.

18. From the unmanifest all manifestations
  Come forth at the coming of (Brahman's) day,
And dissolve at the coming of night,
  In that same one, known as the unmanifest.

19. This very same host of beings,
  Coming into existence over and over, is dissolved
At the approach of night, willy-nilly, son of Pṛthā,
  And comes forth at the approach of day.

20. But higher than that is another state of being,
  Unmanifest, (higher) than (that) unmanifest, eternal,
Which when all beings
  Perish, perishes not.

21. (This) unmanifest is called the indestructible;
  It they call the highest goal,
Attaining which they return not;
  That is My highest station.[6]

22. This is the supreme Spirit, son of Pṛthā,
  To be won, however, by unswerving devotion;
Within which (all) beings are fixed,
  By which this universe is pervaded.

23. But at what times to non-return,
  And (when) to return, disciplined men
Dying depart, those times
  I shall declare, bull of Bharatas.[7]

24. Fire, light, day, the bright (lunar fortnight),
  The six months that are the northward course of the sun,
Dying in these, go
  To Brahman Brahman-knowing folk.

25. Smoke, night, also the dark (lunar fortnight),
  The six months that are the southward course of the sun,
In these (when he dies) to the moon's light
  Attaining, the disciplined man returns.

26. For these two paths, light and dark,
  Are held to be eternal for the world;
By one, man goes to non-return,
  By the other he returns again.

27. Knowing these two paths, son of Pṛthā, not
    Is any disciplined man confused.
  Therefore at all times
    Be disciplined in discipline, Arjuna.

28. In the Vedas, in acts of worship, and in austerities,
    In alms-gifts, what fruit of merit is ordained,
  All that surpasses he who knows this,
    The man of discipline, and goes to the highest primal place.

Here ends the Eighth Chapter, called Discipline of the Imperishable Brahman.

CHAPTER IX

The Blessed One said:

1. But this most secret thing to thee
   I shall declare, since thou cavillest not,
This theoretical knowledge joined with practical,[1]
   Knowing which thou shalt be freed from evil.

2. A royal science, a royal mystery,
   A supreme purifier is this,
Immediately comprehensible, righteous,
   Easy to carry out, imperishable.

3. Men who put no faith
   In this religious truth, scorcher of the foe,
Do not attain Me, and return
   On the path of the endless round of deaths.

4. By Me is pervaded all this
   Universe, by Me in the form of the unmanifest.
All beings rest in Me,
   And I do not rest in them.

5. And (yet) beings do not rest in Me:
   Behold My divine mystery (or magic)!
Supporter of beings, and not resting in beings,
   Is My Self, that causes beings to be.

6. As constantly abides in the ether
   The great wind, that penetrates everywhere,
So all beings
   Abide in Me; make sure of that.

7. All beings, son of Kuntī,
   Pass into My material nature
At the end of a world-eon; them again
   I send forth at the beginning of a (new) world-eon.

8. Taking as base My own material-nature
   I send forth again and again
This whole host of beings,
   Which is powerless, by the power of (My) material nature.

9. And Me these actions do not
Bind, Dhanaṃjaya, —
Sitting in as one sitting out (participating as one indifferent),
Unattached to these actions.

10. With Me as overseer, material nature
Brings forth (the world of) moving and unmoving (beings);
By this motive-force, son of Kuntī,
The world goes around.

11. Fools despise Me
That have assumed human form,
Not knowing the higher state
Of Me, which is the great lord of beings.

12. They are of vain aspirations, of vain actions,
Of vain knowledge, bereft of insight;
In ogrish and demoniac
Nature, which is delusive, they abide.

13. But 'tis Me, son of Pṛthā, that great-souled men,
Abiding in god-like nature,
Revere with unswerving thoughts,
Knowing (Me as) the beginning of beings, the imperishable.

14. Ever glorifying Me,
And striving with firm resolve,
And paying homage to Me with devotion,
Constantly disciplined, they wait upon Me.

15. With knowledge-worship also others
Worshiping wait upon Me,
In My unique and manifold forms,
(Me as) variously (manifested), facing in all directions.

16. I am the ritual act, I am the act of worship,
I am the offering to the dead, I am the medicinal herb,
I am the sacred formula, I alone am the sacrificial butter,
I am the fire of offering, I am the poured oblation.

17. I am the father of this world,
The mother, the establisher, the grandsire,
The object of knowledge, the purifier, the sacred syllable *om*,
The verse of praise, the chant, and the sacrificial formula;

18. The goal, supporter, lord, witness,
    The dwelling-place, refuge, friend,
The origin, dissolution, and maintenance,
    The treasure-house, the imperishable seed.

19. I give heat; the rain I
    Hold back and send forth;
Both immortality and death,
    Both the existent and the non-existent am I, Arjuna.

20. The three-Veda-men, soma-drinkers, purified of sin, Me
    With ritual worship worshiping, seek to go to heaven;
They, attaining the meritorious world of the lord of the gods (Indra),
    Taste in the sky the divine enjoyments of the gods.

21. They, after enjoying the expansive world of heaven,
    When their merit is exhausted, enter the world of mortals;
Thus conforming to the religion of the three (Vedas),
    Men who lust after desires get that which comes and goes.

22. Thinking on Me, with no other thought,
    What folk wait upon Me,
To them, when they are constant in perseverance,
    I bring acquisition and peaceful possession (of their aim).

23. Even those who are devotees of other gods,
    And worship them permeated with faith,
It is only Me, son of Kuntī, that even they
    Worship, (tho) not in the enjoined fashion.

24. For I of all acts of worship
    Am both the recipient and the lord;
But they do not recognize Me
    In the true way; therefore they fall (from the 'heaven' they win).

25. Votaries of the gods go to the gods,
    Votaries of the (departed) fathers go to the fathers,
Worshipers of goblins go to the goblins,
    Worshipers of Me also go to Me.

26. A leaf, a flower, a fruit, or water,
    Who presents to Me with devotion,
That offering of devotion I
    Accept from the devout-souled (giver).[2]

27. Whatever thou doest, whatever thou eatest,
Whatever thou offerest in oblation or givest,
Whatever austerity thou performest, son of Kuntī,
That do as an offering to Me.

28. Thus from what have good and evil fruits
Thou shalt be freed, (namely) from the bonds of action;
Thy soul disciplined in the discipline of renunciation,[3]
Freed, thou shalt go to Me.

29. I am the same to all beings,
No one is hateful or dear to Me;
But those who revere Me with devotion,
They are in Me and I too am in them.

30. Even if a very evil doer
Reveres Me with single devotion,
He must be regarded as righteous in spite of all;
For he has the right resolution.

31. Quickly his soul becomes righteous,
And he goes to eternal peace.
Son of Kuntī, make sure of this:
No devotee of Mine is lost.

32. For if they take refuge in Me, son of Pṛthā,
Even those who may be of base origin,
Women, men of the artisan caste, and serfs too,
Even they go to the highest goal.

33. How much more virtuous brahmans,
And devout royal seers, too!
A fleeting and joyless world
This; having attained it, devote thyself to Me.

34. Be Me-minded, devoted to Me;
Worshiping Me, pay homage to Me;
Just to Me shalt thou go, having thus disciplined
Thyself, fully intent on Me.

Here ends the Ninth Chapter, called Discipline of Royal Knowledge and Royal Mystery.

CHAPTER X

The Blessed One said:

1. Yet further, great-armed one,
   Hear My highest message,
Which to thee, that delightest in it, I
   Shall declare, in that I wish thee well.

2. The throngs of gods know not My
   Origin, nor yet the great seers.
For I am the starting-point of the gods,
   And of the great seers, altogether.

3. Whoso Me the unborn and beginningless
   Knows, the great lord of the world,
Undeluded, he among mortals
   Is freed from all evils.

4. Enlightenment, knowledge, non-delusion,
   Patience, truth, control, peace,
Pleasure, pain, arising, passing away,
   Fear, and fearlessness too,

5. Harmlessness, indifference, content,
   Austerity, generosity, fame and ill repute —
(All) conditions of beings arise
   From Me alone, however various their nature.

6. The seven great seers of old,
   The four Manus [1] likewise,
Originate from Me,[2] as My mental offspring,
   From whom spring these creatures in the world.

7. This supernal-manifestation [3] and mystic power
   Of Mine, whoso knows in very truth —
He with unswerving discipline
   Is disciplined; there is no doubt of that.

8. I am the origin of all;
   From Me all comes forth.
Knowing this they revere Me,
   Enlightened men, pervaded with (the proper) state (of mind).[4]

9. With thoughts on Me, with life concentrated on Me,
Enlightening one another,
And telling constantly of Me,
They find contentment and joy.

10. To them, constantly disciplined,
Revering Me with love,
I give that discipline of mind,
Whereby they go unto Me.

11. To show compassion to those same ones,
Their ignorance-born darkness I
Dispel, (while) remaining in My own true state,
With the shining light of knowledge.

Arjuna said:

12. The supreme Brahman, the supreme station,[5]
The supreme purifier art Thou!
The eternal divine spirit,
The primal deity, the unborn lord,[6]

13. Call Thee all the seers,
And the divine seer Nārada,
Asita Devala,[7] and Vyāsa,
And Thou Thyself declarest it to me.

14. All this I hold to be true,
Which Thou sayest to me, Keśava;
For Thy manifestation, Blessed One, neither
The gods nor the demons know.

15. Thine own self by Thy self alone
Knowest Thou, highest of spirits,
Cause of being of beings, lord of beings,
God of gods, lord of the world.

16. Declare then fully, I pray Thee, —
For marvelous are the supernal-manifestations of Thy self,
With which manifestations the worlds
Here pervading Thou abidest ever.

17. How may I know Thee, Thou of mystic power,
Ever meditating on Thee?
And in what several states of being
Art Thou to be thought of by me, Blessed One?

18. In full detail, Thine own mystic power
    And supernal-manifestation, Janārdana,
Expound further; for satiety
    Comes not to me as I listen to Thy nectar!

Thy Blessed One said:

19. Come then, I shall tell thee —
    Since My supernal-manifestations are marvelous[8] —
Regarding the chief ones, best of Kurus;
    There is no end to My extent.

20. I am the soul, Guḍākeśa,
    That abides in the heart of all beings;
I am the beginning and the middle
    Of beings, and the very end too.

21. Of the Ādityas I am Viṣṇu,
    Of lights the radiant sun,
Of Maruts I am (their chief) Marīci,
    Of stars I am the moon.

22. Of Vedas I am the Sāma Veda,
    Of gods I am Vāsava (Indra),
Of sense-organs I am the thought-organ,
    Of beings I am the intellect.

23. And of Rudras I am Śaṃkara (Śiva),
    Of sprites and ogres I am the Lord of Wealth (Kubera),
Of (the eight) Vasus I am the Fire(-god),
    Of mountain-peaks I am Meru.

24. Of house-priests the chief am I,
    Bṛhaspati (the priest-god), know thou, son of Pṛthā;
Of army-lords I am Skanda (god of war),
    Of bodies of water I am the ocean.

25. Of great sages I am Bhṛgu,
    Of utterances I am the one syllable (*om*),
Of acts of worship I am the muttered worship,
    Of mountain-ranges Himālaya.

26. The holy fig-tree of all trees,
    Of divine sages Nārada,
Of gandharvas (heavenly musicians), Citraratha (their chief),
    Of perfected beings, the seer Kapila.

27. Uccaiḥśravas (Indra's steed) of horses,
Sprung from the nectar (churned out of ocean), know Me to be;
Of princely elephants, Airāvata (Indra's elephant),
And of men, the king.

28. Of weapons I am (Indra's) vajra,
Of cows I am the Cow-of-Wishes,
I am the generating Kandarpa (god of love),
Of serpents I am (the serpent-king) Vāsuki.

29. And I am Ananta of the Nāgas (fabulous serpents),
I am Varuṇa (god of water) of water-creatures,
Of (departed) fathers I am (their chief god) Aryaman,
I am Yama (god of death) of subduers.[9]

30. Of demons I am (their prince) Prahlāda,
I am Time of impellent-forces,[10]
Of beasts I am the king of beasts,[11]
I am the son of Vinatā (Garuḍa, Viṣṇu's bird) of birds.

31. I am the wind of purifiers,
Rāma of warriors,
I am the dolphin of water-monsters,
Of rivers I am the Ganges.

32. Of creations the beginning and the end,
And the middle too am I, Arjuna;
Of knowledges the knowledge of the over-soul,
I am speech of them that speak.[12]

33. Of syllables (letters) I am the letter A,
And the dvandva of compounds,
None but I am immortal Time,
I am the Ordainer (Creator) with faces in all directions.

34. I am death that carries off all,
And the origin of things that are to be;
Of feminine entities I am Fame, Fortune, Speech,
Memory, Wisdom, Steadfastness, Patience.[13]

35. Likewise of chants the Great Chant,
The Gāyatrī am I of meters,
Of months, (the first month) Mārgaśīrṣa am I,
Of seasons the flower-bearer (spring).

36. I am gambling of rogues,
   I am majesty of the majestic,
I am conquest, I am the spirit-of-adventure,
   I am courage of the courageous.[14]

37. Of the Vṛṣṇi-clansmen I am Vāsudeva,
   Of the sons of Pāṇḍu, Dhanaṃjaya (Arjuna),
Of hermits also I am Vyāsa,
   Of sages the sage Uśanas.

38. I am the rod (punitive force) of stern controllers,
   I am statecraft of them that seek political success;
Taciturnity too am I of secret things,
   I am knowledge of the knowing.

39. Moreover whatsoever of all beings
   Is the seed, that am I, Arjuna;
There is none such as could be without
   Me, no being moving or unmoving.

40. There is no end to My marvelous
   Supernal-manifestations, scorcher of the foe;
But I have now declared by way of examples
   The extent of my supernal-manifestation.

41. Whatever being shows supernal-manifestations,[15]
   Or majesty or vigor,
Be thou assured that that in every case
   Is sprung from a fraction of My glory.

42. After all, this extensive
   Instruction — what boots it thee, Arjuna?
I support this entire
   World with a single fraction (of Myself), and remain so.

Here ends the Tenth Chapter, called Discipline of Supernal-Manifestations.

CHAPTER XI

Arjuna said:

1. As a favor to me the supreme
   Mystery, called the over-soul,
   The words which Thou hast spoken, thereby
   This delusion of mine is dispelled.

2. For the origin and dissolution of beings
   Have been heard by me in full detail
   From Thee, Lotus-petal-eyed One,
   And also (Thine) exalted nature unending.

3. Thus it is, as Thou declarest
   Thyself, O Supreme Lord.
   I desire to see Thy form
   As God, O Supreme Spirit!

4. If Thou thinkest that it can
   Be seen by me, O Lord,
   Prince of mystic power, then do Thou to me
   Reveal Thine immortal Self.

The Blessed One said:

5. Behold My forms, son of Pṛthā,
   By hundreds and by thousands,
   Of various sorts, marvelous,
   Of various colors and shapes.

6. Behold the Ādityas, Vasus, Rudras,
   The Aśvin-pair and the Maruts too;
   Many before-unseen
   Marvels behold, son of Bharata.

7. Here the whole world united
   Behold today, with moving and unmoving things,
   In My body, Guḍākeśa,
   And whatsoever else thou wishest to see.

8. But thou canst not see Me
   With this same eye of thine own;
   I give thee a supernatural eye:
   Behold My mystic power as God!

Saṃjaya said:

9. Thus speaking then, O king,
Hari (Viṣṇu), the great Lord of Mystic Power,
Showed unto the son of Pṛthā
His supernal form as God:

10. Of many mouths and eyes,
Of many wondrous aspects,
Of many marvelous ornaments,
Of marvelous and many uplifted weapons;

11. Wearing marvelous garlands and garments,
With marvelous perfumes and ointments,
Made up of all wonders, the god,
Infinite, with faces in all directions.

12. Of a thousand suns in the sky
If suddenly should burst forth
The light, it would be like
Unto the light of that exalted one.

13. The whole world there united,
And divided many-fold,
Beheld in the God of Gods'
Body the son of Pāṇḍu then.

14. Then filled with amazement,
His hair standing upright, Dhanaṃjaya
Bowed with his head to the God,
And said with a gesture of reverence:

Arjuna said:

15. I see the gods in Thy body, O God,
All of them, and the hosts of various kinds of beings too,
Lord Brahmā sitting on the lotus-seat,
And the seers all, and the divine serpents.

16. With many arms, bellies, mouths, and eyes,
I see Thee, infinite in form on all sides;
No end nor middle nor yet beginning of Thee
Do I see, O All-God, All-formed!

17. With diadem, club, and disc,
A mass of radiance, glowing on all sides,
I see Thee, hard to look at, on every side
With the glory of flaming fire and sun, immeasurable.

18. Thou art the Imperishable, the supreme Object of Knowledge;
Thou art the ultimate resting-place[1] of this universe;
Thou art the immortal guardian of the eternal right,
Thou art the everlasting Spirit, I hold.

19. Without beginning, middle, or end, of infinite power,
Of infinite arms, whose eyes are the moon and sun,
I see Thee, whose face[2] is flaming fire,
Burning this whole universe with Thy radiance.

20. For this region between heaven and earth
Is pervaded by Thee alone, and all the directions;
Seeing this Thy wondrous, terrible form,
The triple world trembles, O exalted one!

21. For into Thee are entering[3] yonder throngs of gods;
Some, affrighted, praise Thee with reverent gestures;
Crying 'Hail!' the throngs of the great seers and perfected ones
Praise Thee with abundant laudations.

22. The Rudras, the Ādityas, the Vasus, and the Sādhyas,
All-gods, Aśvins, Maruts, and the Steam-drinkers ('fathers'),
The hosts of heavenly musicians, sprites, demons, and perfected ones,
Gaze upon Thee, and all are quite amazed.

23. Thy great form, of many mouths and eyes,
O great-armed one, of many arms, thighs, and feet,
Of many bellies, terrible with many tusks, —
Seeing it the worlds tremble, and I too.

24. Touching the sky, aflame, of many colors,
With yawning mouths and flaming enormous eyes,
Verily seeing Thee (so), my inmost soul is shaken,
And I find no steadiness nor peace, O Viṣṇu!

25. And Thy mouths, terrible with great tusks,
No sooner do I see them, like the fire of dissolution (of the world),
Than I know not the directions of the sky, and I find no refuge;
Have mercy, Lord of Gods, Thou in whom the world dwells!

26. And Thee[4] yonder sons of Dhṛtarāṣṭra,
All of them, together with the hosts of kings,
Bhīṣma, Droṇa, and yonder son of the charioteer (Karṇa) too,
Together with our chief warriors likewise,

27. Hastening enter Thy mouths,
  Frightful with tusks, and terrifying;
Some, stuck between the teeth,
  Are seen with their heads crushed.

28. As the many water-torrents of the rivers
  Rush headlong towards the single sea,
So yonder heroes of the world of men into Thy
  Flaming mouths do enter.

29. As moths into a burning flame
  Do enter unto their destruction with utmost impetuosity,
Just so unto their destruction enter the worlds [5]
  Into Thy mouths also, with utmost impetuosity.

30. Devouring them Thou lickest up voraciously on all sides
  All the worlds with Thy flaming jaws;
Filling with radiance the whole universe,
  Thy terrible splendors burn, O Viṣṇu!

31. Tell me, who art Thou, of awful form?
  Homage be to Thee: Best of Gods, be merciful!
I desire to understand Thee, the primal one;
  For I do not comprehend what Thou hast set out to do.

The Blessed One said:

32. I am Time (Death), cause of destruction of the worlds, matured
  And set out to gather in the worlds here.
Even without thee (thy action), all shall cease to exist,
  The warriors that are drawn up in the opposing ranks.

33. Therefore arise thou, win glory,
  Conquer thine enemies and enjoy prospered kingship;
By Me Myself they have already been slain long ago;
  Be thou the mere instrument, left-handed archer!

34. Droṇa and Bhīṣma and Jayadratha,
  Karṇa too, and the other warrior-heroes as well,
Do thou slay, (since) they are already slain by Me; do not hesitate!
  Fight! Thou shalt conquer thy rivals in battle.

Saṃjaya said:

35. Hearing these words of Keśava,
  Making a reverent gesture, trembling, the Diademed (Arjuna)
Made obeisance and spoke yet again to Kṛṣṇa,
  Stammering, greatly affrighted, bowing down:

Arjuna said:

36. It is in place, Hṛṣīkeśa, that at Thy praise
The world rejoices and is exceeding glad;
Ogres fly in terror in all directions,
And all the hosts of perfected ones pay homage.

37. And why should they not pay homage to Thee, Exalted One?
Thou art greater even than Brahman [6]; Thou art the First Creator;
O infinite Lord of Gods, in whom the world dwells,
Thou the imperishable, existent, non-existent, and beyond both!

38. Thou art the Primal God, the Ancient Spirit,
Thou art the supreme resting-place [7] of this universe;
Thou art the knower, the object of knowledge, and the highest station,
By Thee the universe is pervaded, Thou of infinite form!

39. Vāyu, Yama, Agni, Varuṇa, the moon,
Prajāpati art Thou, and the Greatgrandsire;
Homage, homage be to Thee a thousand fold,
And again be yet further homage, homage to Thee!

40. Homage be to Thee from in front and from behind,
Homage be to Thee from all sides, Thou All!
O Thou of infinite might,[8] Thy prowess is unmeasured;
Thou attainest all; therefore Thou art All!

41. Whatever I said rashly, thinking Thee my boon-companion,
Calling Thee 'Kṛṣṇa, Yādava, Companion!,'
Not knowing this (truth, namely) Thy greatness,
Thru careless negligence, or even thru affection,

42. And if I treated Thee disrespectfully, to make sport of Thee,
In the course of amusement, resting, sitting, or eating,
Either alone, O unshaken one, or in the presence of those (others),
For that I beg forgiveness of Thee, the immeasurable one.

43. Thou art the father of the world of things that move and move not,
And Thou art its revered, most venerable Guru;
There is no other like Thee — how then a greater? —
Even in the three worlds, O Thou of matchless greatness!

44. Therefore, bowing and prostrating my body,
I beg grace of Thee, the Lord to be revered:
As a father to his son, as a friend to his friend,
As a lover to his beloved, be pleased to show mercy, O God!

45. Having seen what was never seen before, I am thrilled,
And (at the same time) my heart is shaken with fear;
Show me, O God, that same form of Thine (as before)!
Be merciful, Lord of Gods, Abode of the World!

46. Wearing the diadem, carrying the club, with disc in hand,
Just (as before) I desire to see Thee;
In that same four-armed shape
Present Thyself, O Thousand-armed One, of universal form!

The Blessed One said:

47. By Me showing grace towards thee, Arjuna, this
Supreme form has been manifested by My own mysterious power;
(This form) made up of splendor, universal, infinite, primal,
Of Mine, which has never been seen before by any other than thee.

48. Not by the Vedas, by acts of worship, or study, or gifts,
Nor yet by rites, nor by grim austerities,
In the world of men can I in such a form
Be seen by any other than thee, hero of the Kurus.

49. Have no perturbation, nor any state of bewilderment,
Seeing this so awful form of Mine;
Dispel thy fear; let thy heart be of good cheer; again do thou
Behold that same (former) form of Mine: here!

Saṃjaya said:

50. Having thus spoken to Arjuna, Vāsudeva
Again revealed his own (natural) form,
And comforted him in his fright
By once more assuming his gracious aspect, the Exalted One.

Arjuna said:

51. Seeing this human form
Of Thine, gracious, O Janārdana,
Now I have become
Possessed of my senses, and restored to normal state.

The Blessed One said:

52. This form that is right hard to see,
Which thou hast seen of Mine,
Of this form even the gods
Constantly long for the sight.

53. Not by the Vedas nor by austerity,
Nor by gifts or acts of worship,
Can I be seen in such a guise,
As thou hast seen Me.

54. But by unswerving devotion can
I in such a guise, Arjuna,
Be known and seen in very truth,
And entered into, scorcher of the foe.

55. Doing My work, intent on Me,
Devoted to Me, free from attachment,
Free from enmity to all beings,
Who is so, goes to Me, son of Pāṇḍu.

Here ends the Eleventh Chapter, called Discipline of the Vision of the Universal Form.

CHAPTER XII

Arjuna said:

1. Those who are thus constantly disciplined,
   And revere Thee with devotion,
   And those also who (revere) the imperishable unmanifest —
   Of these which are the best knowers of discipline?

The Blessed One said:

2. Fixing the thought-organ on Me, those who Me
   Revere with constant discipline,
   Pervaded with supreme faith,
   Them I hold to be the most disciplined.

3. But those who the imperishable, undefinable,
   Unmanifest, revere,
   The omnipresent and unthinkable,
   The immovable,[1] unchanging, fixed,

4. Restraining the throng of the senses,
   With mental attitude alike to all,[2]
   They (also) reach none but Me,
   Delighting in the welfare of all beings.

5. Greater is the toil of them
   That have their hearts fixed on the unmanifest;
   For with difficulty is the unmanifest goal
   Attained by embodied (souls).

6. But those who, all actions
   Casting on Me, intent on Me,
   With utterly unswerving discipline
   Meditating on Me, revere Me,

7. For them I the Savior
   From the sea of the round of deaths
   Become right soon, son of Pṛthā,
   When they have made their thoughts enter into Me.

8. Fix thy thought-organ on Me alone;
   Make thy consciousness enter into Me;
   And thou shalt come to dwell even in Me
   Hereafter; there is no doubt of this.

9. But if to fix thy thought
Steadfastly on Me thou art not able,
With the discipline of practice then
Seek to win Me, Dhanaṃjaya.

10. If thou hast no ability even for practice,
Be wholly devoted to work for Me;
For My sake also actions
Performing, thou shalt win perfection.

11. But if even this thou art unable
To do, resorting to My discipline,
Abandonment of the fruit of all actions
Do thou then effect, controlling thyself.

12. For knowledge is better than practice,
And meditation is superior to knowledge,
And abandonment of the fruit of actions is better than meditation;
From abandonment (comes) peace immediately.

13. No hater of all beings,
Friendly and compassionate,
Free from selfishness and I-faculty,
Indifferent to pain and pleasure, patient,

14. The disciplined man who is always content,
Whose self is controlled, of firm resolve,
Whose thought and consciousness are fixed on Me,
Who is devoted to Me, he is dear to Me.

15. He before whom people do not tremble,
And who does not tremble before people,
From joy, impatience, fear, and agitation
Who is free, he too is dear to Me.

16. Unconcerned, pure, capable,
Disinterested, free from perturbation,
Abandoning all undertakings,
Who is devoted to Me, is dear to Me.

17. Who neither delights nor loathes,
Neither grieves nor craves,
Renouncing good and evil (objects),
Who is full of devotion, he is dear to Me.

18. Alike to foe and friend,
    Also to honor and disgrace,
To cold and heat, joy and sorrow
    Alike, freed from attachment,

19. To whom blame and praise are equal, restrained in speech,
    Content with anything that comes,
Having no home, of steadfast mind,
    Full of devotion, that man is dear to Me.

20. But those who this nectar [3] of duty
    Revere as it has (now) been declared,
Having faith (in it), intent on Me,
    Those devotees are beyond measure dear to Me.

Here ends the Twelfth Chapter, Called Discipline of Devotion.

CHAPTER XIII

The Blessed One said:

1. This body, son of Kuntī,
   Is called the Field.
   Who knows this, he is called
   Field-knower by those who know him.

2. Know also that I am the Field-knower
   In all Fields, son of Bharata.
   Knowledge of the Field and Field-knower,
   This I hold to be (true) knowledge.

3. This Field, what it is and of what nature,
   What its modifications, and whence which one (is derived),
   And who He (the Field-knower) is, and what His powers are,
   That hear from Me in brief.

4. This has been sung in many ways by the seers
   In various (Vedic [1]) hymns severally,
   And also in words of aphorisms about Brahman (in the Upaniṣads[2]),
   Well-reasoned and definite.

5. The gross elements, the I-faculty,
   The consciousness, and the unmanifest,
   The senses ten and one,
   And the five objects on which the senses (of perception) play,

6. Desire, loathing, pleasure, pain,
   Association,[3] intellect, steadfastness,
   This in brief as the Field
   Is described, with its modifications.

7. Absence of pride and deceit,
   Harmlessness, patience, uprightness,
   Service of a teacher, purity,
   Firmness, self-control,

8. Aversion to the objects of sense,
   And absence of I-faculty;
   As regards birth, death, old age, disease,
   And sorrow, a perception of their evils;

9. Absence of attachment and of great affection
For sons, wife, house, and the like,
And constant indifference of mind,
Whether desired or undesired things occur;

10. With single-minded discipline, towards Me
Devotion unswerving;
Cultivation of solitary places,
Dislike for a crowd of people;

11. Constancy in the knowledge of the over-soul,
Perception of the object [4] of knowledge of the truth: —
This (all) is called knowledge;
Ignorance is what is other than that.

12. What is the object of knowledge, that I shall declare,
Knowing which one attains freedom from death:
(It is) the beginningless Brahman, ruled by Me[5];
Neither existent nor non-existent it is called.

13. It has hands and feet on all sides,
Eyes, heads, and faces [6] on all sides,
Hearing [7] on all sides in the world,
And it remains constantly enveloping all;

14. Having the semblance [8] of the qualities of all the senses,
(Yet) freed from all the senses,
Unattached, and yet all-maintaining;
Free from the Strands, yet experiencing the Strands (of matter);

15. Outside of beings, and within them,
Unmoving, and yet moving;
Because of its subtleness it cannot be comprehended:
Both far away and near it is.

16. Both undivided in beings,
And seemingly divided it remains;
Both as the supporter of beings it is to be known,
And as (their) consumer and originator.

17. Of lights also it is the light [9]
Beyond darkness, so 'tis declared;
Knowledge, the object of knowledge, and the goal of knowledge; [10]
(It is) settled [11] in the heart of all.

18. Thus the Field, and also knowledge,
And the object of knowledge have been declared in brief;
My devotee, understanding this,
Attains unto [12] My estate.

19. Both material nature and the spirit,
Know thou, are equally beginningless;
Both the modifications and the Strands,
Know thou, spring from material nature.

20. In anything that concerns effect, instrument, or agent,[13]
Material nature is declared the cause;
The spirit, in pleasure-and-pain's
Experiencing is declared the cause.

21. For the spirit, abiding in material nature,
Experiences the Strands born of material nature;
Attachment to the Strands is the cause of his
Births in good and evil wombs.

22. The onlooker and consenter,
The supporter, experiencer, great Lord,
The supreme soul also is declared to be
The highest spirit, in this body.

23. Whoso thus knows the spirit
And material nature along with its Strands,
Tho he exist in any condition at all,[14]
He is not reborn again.

24. By meditation, in the self see
Some the self by the self;
Others by discipline of reason,[15]
And others by discipline of action.

25. But others, not having this knowledge,
Hearing it from others, revere it;
Even they also, nevertheless, cross over
Death, devoted to the holy revelation [16] which they hear.

26. In so far as is produced any
Creature, stationary or moving,
From union of Field and Field-knower
Know that (is sprung), best of Bharatas.

27. Alike in all beings
Abiding, the supreme Lord,
Not perishing when they perish,
Who sees him, he (truly) sees.

28. For seeing in all the same
Lord established,
He harms not himself (in others)[17] by himself;
Then he goes to the highest goal.

29. Both that by material-nature alone actions
Are performed altogether,
Who sees, and likewise that (his) self
Is not the doer, he (truly) sees.

30. When the various states of beings
He perceives as abiding in One,
And from that alone their expansion,
Then he attains Brahman.

31. Because he is beginningless and free from the Strands,
This supreme self, imperishable,
Even abiding in the body, son of Kuntī,
Acts not, nor is he stained (by actions).

32. As because of its subtleness the omnipresent
Ether is not stained (by contact with other elements),
Abiding in every body
The self is not stained likewise.

33. As alone illumines
This whole world the sun,
So the Field-owner the whole Field
Illumines, son of Bharata.

34. Thus between Field and Field-knower
The difference, with the eye of knowledge,
And release from the material nature of beings,
Those who know (these), they go to the highest.

Here ends the Thirteenth Chapter, called Discipline of Distinction of Field and Field-knower.

CHAPTER XIV

The Blessed One said:

1. Further I shall declare the highest
   Knowledge, the best of all knowledges,
Knowing which all saints
   Have gone from this world to supreme perfection.

2. Having resorted to this knowledge,
   Come to a state of likeness with Me,
Even at a world-creation they do not come to birth,
   Nor at a dissolution are they disturbed.

3. For Me great Brahman is a womb;
   Therein I plant the germ;
The origin of all beings
   Comes from that, son of Bharata.

4. In all wombs, son of Kuntī,
   Whatsoever forms originate,
Of them great Brahman is the womb,
   I am the father that furnishes the seed.

5. Goodness, passion, and darkness,
   The Strands that spring from material nature,
Bind, O great-armed one,
   In the body the immortal embodied (soul).

6. Among these goodness, because it is stainless,
   Is illuminating and free from disease;
It binds by attachment to bliss,
   And by attachment to knowledge, blameless one.

7. Know that passion is of the nature of desire,
   Springing from thirst and attachment;
It, son of Kuntī, binds
   The embodied (soul) by attachment to actions.

8. But know that darkness is born of ignorance,
   The deluder of all embodied (souls);
By heedlessness, sloth, and sleep
   It binds, son of Bharata.

9. Goodness causes attachment to bliss,
   Passion to action, son of Bharata,
But darkness, obscuring knowledge,
   Causes attachment to heedlessness likewise.

10. Prevailing over passion and darkness,
   Goodness comes to be, son of Bharata;
Passion, (prevailing over) goodness and darkness likewise,
   And so darkness, (prevailing over) goodness and passion.

11. In all the gates (orifices) in this body
   An illumination appears,
Which is knowledge; when that happens, then one shall know
   Also that goodness is dominant,

12. Greed, activity, the undertaking
   Of actions, unrest, longing,
These are produced when passion
   Is dominant, bull of Bharatas.

13. Unillumination, and inactivity,
   Heedlessness, and mere delusion,
These are produced when darkness
   Is dominant, son of Kuru.

14. But when under dominance of goodness
   The body-bearing (soul) goes to dissolution,
Then to the worlds of them that know the highest,
   The spotless (worlds), he attains.

15. Going to dissolution in (dominance of) passion,
   He is born among those attached to actions;
And so when dissolved in (dominance of) darkness,
   He is born in deluded wombs.

16. Of action well done, they say
   The fruit is spotless and of the nature of goodness;
But the fruit of passion is pain;
   The fruit of darkness is ignorance.

17. From goodness is born knowledge,
   From passion greed rather,
Heedlessness and delusion from darkness
   Arise, and ignorance.

18. Those that abide in goodness go on high;
The men of passion remain in the middle (states);
Abiding in the scope of the base Strand,
The men of darkness go below.

19. No other agent than the Strands
When the Beholder (soul) perceives,
And knows the higher-than-the-Strands,
He goes unto My estate.

20. Transcending these three Strands,
That spring from the body,[1] the embodied (soul),
From birth, death, old age, and sorrow
Freed, attains deathlessness.

Arjuna said:

21. By what marks, when these three Strands
He has transcended, is he characterized, O Lord?
What is his conduct, and how these
Three Strands does he get beyond?

The Blessed One said:

22. Both illumination and activity
And delusion,[2] son of Pāṇḍu,
He does not loathe when they have arisen,
Nor crave when they have ceased.

23. Sitting as one sitting apart (indifferent),
Who is not perturbed by the Strands,
Thinking 'The Strands operate' only,
Who remains firm and is unshaken,

24. To whom pain and pleasure are alike, abiding in the self,
To whom clods, stones, and gold are all one,
To whom loved and unloved are equal, wise,[3]
To whom blame and praise of himself are equal,

25. Alike to honor and disgrace,
Alike to parties of friend and foe,
Abandoning all undertakings,
He is called the man that has transcended the Strands.

26. And whoso Me with unswerving
    Discipline of devotion serves,
He, transcending these Strands,
    Is fit for becoming Brahman.

27. For I am the foundation of Brahman,
    The immortal and imperishable,
And of the eternal right,
    And of absolute bliss.

Here ends the Fourteenth Chapter, called Discipline of Distinction of the Three Strands.

CHAPTER XV

The Blessed One said:

1. With roots aloft and branches below,
   The eternal peepal-tree,[1] they say —
Whose leaves are the (Vedic) hymns,
   Who knows it, he knows the Veda.

2. Below and upward extend its branches,
   Nourished by the Strands, with the objects of sense as sprouts;
Below also are stretched forth its roots,
   Resulting in actions, in the world of men.

3. Its form is not thus comprehended here in the world,
   Nor its end nor beginning nor basis.
This peepal-tree, with its firmly grown roots,
   Cutting with the stout axe of detachment,

4. Then that place must be sought
   To which having gone men no more return,
(Thinking:) 'I take refuge in that same primal spirit,
   Whence issued forth of old the (whole cosmic) activity.'

5. Without pride or delusion, victors over the sin of attachment,
   Constant in the over-soul, their desires departed,
Freed from the pairs known as pleasure and pain,
   Undeluded men go to that eternal place.

6. The sun does not illumine that,
   Nor the moon, nor fire;
Having gone to which they return not:
   That is My highest station.[2]

7. A part just of Me in the world of the living
   Becomes the individual-soul, the eternal;
The (five) senses, with the thought-organ as sixth,
   Which rest in material nature, it draws along.

8. When he acquires a body,
   And also when he departs (from it), the Lord[3]
Moves taking them along,
   As the wind odors from their home.

9. Hearing, sight, and touch,
 Taste, and smell,
Making use of [4] these, and the thought-organ, he
 Devotes himself to the objects of sense.

10. As he departs (from the body) or remains (in it),
 Or experiences (sense-objects), while attended by the Strands,
Deluded men do not perceive him;
 Those whose eye is knowledge perceive him.

11. Him also men of discipline, earnestly striving,
 Perceive located in their self;
(But) even tho they strive, those whose self is unperfected
 Perceive him not, the fools.

12. The splendor that belongs to the sun,
 Which illumines the whole world,
And that which is in the moon and in fire,
 Know that to be My splendor.

13. And entering into the earth, (all) beings
 I maintain by (My) power;
And I nourish all plants,
 Becoming the juicy soma (sacred plant and moon, identified).

14. I, becoming the (digestive) fire of all men,
 Dwelling in the body of (all) living beings,
In union with the upper and nether breaths
 Cook (digest) their food of all four sorts.

15. I am entered into the heart of every one;
 From Me come memory, knowledge, and disputation;
I alone am that which is to be known by all the Vedas;
 And I am the author of the Upaniṣads and the Vedas' knower.

16. Here in the world are two spirits,
 The perishable, and the imperishable;
The perishable is all beings;
 The imperishable is called the immovable.[5]

17. But there is a highest spirit, other (than this),
 Called the Supreme Soul;
Which, entering into the three worlds,
 Supports them, the undying Lord.

18. Since I transcend the perishable,
    And am higher than the imperishable too,
  Therefore in the world and the Veda I am
    Proclaimed as the highest spirit.

19. The man who, undeluded, thus Me
    Knows as the supreme spirit,
  He knows all, and devotes himself to Me
    With his whole being, son of Bharata.

20. Thus the most secret science
    Has now been declared by Me, blameless one;
  Being enlightened as to this, a man would have true enlightenment,
    And would have done all there is to do, son of Bharata.

Here ends the Fifteenth Chapter, called Discipline of the Highest Spirit.

CHAPTER XVI

The Blessed One said:

1. Fearlessness, purification of essence,
   Steadfastness in the discipline of knowledge,
Generosity, control, and religious worship,
   Study of the Holy Word, austerities, uprightness,

2. Harmlessness, truth, no anger,
   Abandonment,[1] serenity, no backbiting,
Compassion towards creatures, no greedy desire,
   Gentleness, modesty, no fickleness,

3. Majesty, patience, fortitude, purity,
   No injuriousness, no excessive pride,
Are (the qualities) of him that to the divine lot
   Is born, son of Bharata.

4. Hypocrisy, arrogance, overweening pride,
   Wrath, and harshness (of speech) too,
And ignorance, are (the qualities) of him that is born
   To the demoniac lot, son of Pṛthā.

5. The divine lot leads to release,
   The demoniac lot is considered to lead to bondage.
Be not grieved: to the divine lot
   Thou art born, son of Pāṇḍu.

6. There are two creations of beings in this world,
   The divine and the demoniac.
The divine has been explained at length;
   Hear from Me of the demoniac, son of Pṛthā.

7. Both activity and its cessation[2]
   Demoniac folk know not;
Neither purity nor yet good conduct
   Nor truth is found in them.

8. Without truth, without religious basis, they
   Say is the world, without a God,
Not originating in regular mutual causation;
   In short, motivated by desire alone.

9. Holding fast to this view,
   Men of lost souls, of scant intelligence,
Spring up, committing cruel deeds,
   Unto the ruin of the world, noxious folk.

10. Clinging to insatiable desire,
   Filled with hypocrisy, arrogance, and pride,
Thru delusion taking up false notions,
   They proceed with unclean undertakings.

11. To limitless care,
   That lasts until death, they are devoted;
They make the enjoyment of desires their highest aim,
   Convinced that that is all;

12. Bound by hundreds of bonds of longing,
   Devoted to desire and wrath,
In order to enjoy desires, they seek
   Hoardings of wealth by wrong means.

13. 'This have I gained today,
   This desire I shall get,
Mine is this, and mine also this
   Wealth again is going to be;

14. 'Yonder enemy has been slain by me,
   And I shall slay others too;
I am lord, I control enjoyments,
   I am successful, mighty, happy;

15. 'I am rich, of noble birth;
   Who else is like unto me?
I shall sacrifice and give gifts, and rejoice!'
   Thus they say, deluded by ignorance.

16. Led astray by many fancies,
   Enveloped by the snares of delusion,
Intent on the enjoyment of desires,
   They fall to a foul hell.

17. Self-conceited, haughty,
   Full of pride and arrogance of wealth,[3]
They do acts of religious worship in name alone,
   Hypocritically, not according to the (Vedic) injunctions.

18. Egotism, force, pride,
    Desire, and wrath they have taken to,
Me in their own and others' bodies
    Hating, these envious men.

19. These cruel and hateful
    Base men, in the ceaseless round of existences,[4]
These wicked ones, I constantly hurl
    Into demoniac wombs alone.

20. Having come into a demoniac womb,
    Deluded in birth after birth,
Not by any means attaining Me, son of Kuntī,
    Then they go to the lowest goal.

21. This is of hell the threefold
    Gate, and ruins the soul:
Desire, wrath, and greed;
    Hence one should abandon these three.

22. Freed, son of Kuntī, from these
    Three gates of darkness, a man
Does what is good for his soul;
    Then he goes to the highest goal.

23. Whoso neglects the law's injunction,
    And lives according to his own wilful desires,
He does not attain perfection,
    Nor bliss, nor the highest goal.

24. Therefore let the law be thy authority
    In determining what should and should not be done.
Knowing (action) laid down in the law's injunctions,
    Thou shouldst do (such) action in this world.

Here ends the Sixteenth Chapter, called Discipline of Distinction between Divine and Demoniac Lots.

CHAPTER XVII

Arjuna said:

1. Those who, neglecting the law's injunction,
   Perform acts of worship filled with faith, —
   What, however, is their basis, Kṛṣṇa?
   Goodness, or passion, or darkness?

The Blessed One said:

2. Of three kinds is the faith
   Of embodied (souls); it springs from their original nature;
   It is characterized by goodness, or passion,
   Or darkness. Hear how it is!

3. In accord with the essential nature of every man
   Is his faith, son of Bharata.
   Man here is made up of faith;
   As a man's faith is, just so is he.

4. Men of goodness worship the gods,
   Men of passion sprites and ogres,
   To ghosts and the hordes of goblins others,
   The folk of darkness, pay worship.

5. Not enjoined in the law, cruel
   Austerities — folk who practise them,
   Wedded to hypocrisy and egotism,
   Filled with desire, passion, and violence,[1]

6. Starving within the body
   The conglomerate of elements, the fools,
   And (starving) Me Myself, who am within the body,
   Know that they have demoniac resolve.

7. But the food also, of every man
   Beloved, is of three kinds;
   Likewise their worship, austerities, and gifts;
   Hear now the distinction between them.

8. Life, courage, strength, good health,
   Happiness, and satisfaction increasing,
   Tasty, rich, substantial, and heart-gladdening,
   Such foods are beloved of the man of goodness.

9. Pungent, sour, salty, very hot,
Sharp, astringent, heating,
Such foods are desired of the man of passion;
They cause pain, misery, and sickness.

10. Spoiled, its taste lost,
Putrid, and stale,
Leavings, and also filth,
Such food is beloved of the man of darkness.

11. By men who are not desirous of fruits, worship
Which is offered as contemplated by injunctions,
With the thought that it is simply one's duty to offer it, the mind
Concentrating, that is of goodness.

12. But with a view to the fruit,
And also if for mere hypocritical ostentation
It is offered, O best of Bharatas,
That worship know to be of passion.

13. In which no injunction is observed nor food given out,
No holy texts recited nor sacrificial fee paid,
Devoid of faith, such worship
They say is of darkness.

14. To gods, brahmans, reverend elders, and wise men
Respectful homage; purity, uprightness,
Chastity, and harmlessness;
This is called austerity of the body.

15. Words that cause no disturbance,
That are true, and pleasingly beneficial;
Also practice of recitation in study (of sacred texts);
This is called austerity of speech.

16. Serenity of mind, kindliness,
Silence, self-control,
And purification of being, this
Is called austerity of mind.

17. With the highest faith performed,
This threefold austerity, by men
Not seeking fruits and disciplined,
They call (austerity) of goodness.

18. With a view to respect, honor, and reverence,
And with sheer hypocrisy, what austerity
Is performed, that is called in this world
(Austerity) of passion; it is insecure and impermanent.

19. If with deluded notions, or with self-
Torture, austerity is performed,
Or in order to destroy another,
That is declared to be of darkness.

20. The gift which with the mere thought 'One must give!'
Is given to one that does no (return) favor,
At the proper place and time, to a worthy person,
That gift is said to be of goodness.

21. But what in order to get a return favor,
Or with a view to the fruit as well,
Or when it hurts to give, is given,
That gift is said to be of passion.

22. What gift at the wrong place and time
And to unworthy persons is given,
Without (suitable) marks of respect and with contempt,
That is declared to be of darkness,

23. *Om*, *Tat*, *Sat*: thus the designation
Of Brahman,[2] threefold, is recorded.
Thereby brahmans, and Vedas,
And acts of worship were fashioned of old.

24. Therefore after pronouncing *Om*
Acts of worship, gift, and austerity
Are undertaken as prescribed in (Vedic) injunctions
Always on the part of students of Brahman.

25. With *Tat* ('That'), and without aiming
At fruit, acts of worship and austerity
And acts of giving of various sorts
Are performed by men that seek release.

26. In the meaning of 'real' and in the meaning of 'good'
The word *Sat* is employed;
Likewise of a laudable action
The word *Sat* is used, son of Pṛthā.

27. Also in the matter of worship, austerity, and giving,
Steadfastness is called *Sat*;
And action for such purposes as those
Is likewise called *Sat* ('good').

28. Oblation offered or gift given without faith,
Or austerity or action thus performed,
Is called *Asat* (not *Sat*, not good), son of Pṛthā;
It is naught hereafter and naught in this world.

Here ends the Seventeenth Chapter, called Discipline of Distinction of Three Kinds of Faith.

CHAPTER XVIII

Arjuna said:

1. Of renunciation, great-armed one,
   I desire to know the truth,
   And of abandonment, Hṛṣīkeśa,
   Severally, Slayer of Keśin.

The Blessed One said:

2. The renouncing of acts of desire
   Sages call renunciation.
   The abandonment of all action-fruits
   The wise call abandonment.

3. That it must be abandoned as sinful, some
   Wise men say of action;
   That actions of worship, gift, and austerity
   Must not be abandoned, say others.

4. Hear my decision in this matter
   Of abandonment, best of Bharatas;
   For abandonment, O man-tiger,
   Is reputed to be threefold.

5. Actions of worship, gift, and austerity
   Must not be abandoned, but rather performed;
   Worship, gift, and austerity
   Are purifiers of the wise.

6. However, these actions
   With abandonment of attachment and fruits
   Must be performed: this, son of Pṛthā, is My
   Definite and highest judgment.

7. But abandonment of a (religiously) required
   Action is not seemly;
   Abandonment thereof owing to delusion
   Is reputed to be of the nature of darkness.

8. Just because it is troublesome, what action
   One abandons thru fear of bodily affliction,
   Such a man performs an abandonment that is of the nature of passion;
   By no means shall he get any fruit of (this) abandonment.

9. Simply because it ought to be done, when action
   That is (religiously) required is performed, Arjuna,
Abandoning attachment and fruit,
   That abandonment is held to be of goodness.

10. He loathes not disagreeable action,
   Nor does he cling to agreeable (action),
The man of abandonment who is filled with goodness,
   Wise, whose doubts are destroyed.

11. For a body-bearing (soul) can not
   Abandon actions without remainder;
But he who abandons the fruit of action
   Is called the man of (true) abandonment.

12. Undesired, desired, and mixed —
   Threefold is the fruit of action
That ensues after death for those who are not men of abandonment,
   But never for men of renunciation.

13. O great-armed one, these five
   Factors learn from Me,
Which are declared in the reason-method [1] doctrine
   For the effective performance of all actions.

14. The (material) basis, the agent too,
   And the instruments of various sorts,
And the various motions of several kinds,
   And just Fate as the fifth of them.[2]

15. With body, speech, or mind, whatever
   Action a man undertakes,
Whether it be lawful or the reverse,
   These are its five factors.

16. This being so, as agent herein
   Whoso however the self alone
Regards, because his intelligence is imperfect,
   He does not see (truly), the fool.

17. Whose state (of mind) is not egoized,
   Whose intelligence is not stained,
He, even tho he slays these folk,
   Does not slay, and is not bound (by his actions).

18. Knowledge, the object of knowledge, the knower,
    Form the threefold impellent cause of action;
Instrument, action, and the agent,
    Form the threefold summary of action.[3]

19. Knowledge, and action, and the agent
    Are of just three kinds, according to difference of Strands;
So it is declared in the theory of the Strands;[4]
    Hear of them also, how they are.

20. Whereby in all beings one
    Unchanging condition men perceive,
Unmanifold in the manifold,
    Know that that knowledge is of goodness.

21. But what knowledge in various fashion
    Different conditions of various sorts
Sees in all beings,
    Know that that knowledge is of passion.

22. But what knowledge to one — as if it were all —
    Thing to be done is attached, unconcerned with causes,[5]
Not dealing with the true nature of things, and insignificant,
    That is declared to be of darkness.

23. Obligatory, free from attachment,
    Done without desire or loathing,
By one who seeks no fruit from it, action
    Such as this is called of goodness.

24. But action which by one seeking desires,
    Or again by one who is selfish,
Is done, with much weary labor,
    That is declared to be of passion.

25. Consequences, loss, injury (to others),
    And (one's own) human power disregarding,
Owing to delusion, when action is undertaken,
    It is declared to be of darkness.

26. Free from attachment, not talking of himself,
    Full of steadfastness and energy,
Unchanged in success or failure,
    Such an agent is called one of goodness.

27. Passionate, seeking the fruits of action,
Greedy, injurious, impure,
Full of joy and grief, such an agent
Is celebrated as one of passion.

28. Undisciplined, vulgar, arrogant,
Tricky, dishonest, lazy,
Despondent, and procrastinating,
Such an agent is said to be of darkness.

29. The distinction of intelligence and of firmness, also,
Threefold according to the Strands, hear
Fully expounded
In their several forms, Dhanaṃjaya.

30. Activity and cessation from it,
Things to be done and not to be done, danger and security,
Bondage and release, that which knows these
Is the intelligence that is of goodness, son of Pṛthā.

31. Whereby right and unright,
And things to be done and not to be done,
Are understood incorrectly,
That intelligence, son of Pṛthā, is of passion.

32. Right as unright what
Conceives, obscured by darkness,
And all things contrary (to the truth),
That intelligence, son of Pṛthā, is of darkness.

33. The firmness with which one holds fast
The activities of the mind, life-breaths, and senses,
And which is unswerving in discipline,
That firmness is of goodness, son of Pṛthā.

34. But when to religion, love, and wealth
With firmness he holds fast, Arjuna,
With attachment, desirous of the fruits,
That firmness is of passion, son of Pṛthā.

35. Whereby sleep, fear, sorrow,
Despondency, and pride,
The foolish man does not let go,
That firmness is of darkness, son of Pṛthā.

36. But now the threefold happiness
Hear from Me, bull of Bharatas.
That in which he comes to delight thru long practice (only),
And comes to the end of suffering,

37. Which in the beginning is like poison,
But in maturity like nectar,
That is called the happiness of goodness,
Sprung from serenity of soul and of intellect.[6]

38. (Springing) from union of the senses and their objects,
That which in the beginning is like nectar,
In maturity like poison,
That happiness is recorded as of passion.

39. Which both in the beginning and in its consequence
Is a happiness that deludes the self,
Arising from sleep, sloth, and heedlessness,
That is declared to be of darkness.

40. There is no thing, whether on earth,
Or yet in heaven, among the gods,
No being which free from the material-nature-born
Strands, these three, might be.

41. Of brahmans, warriors, and artisans,
And of serfs, scorcher of the foe,
The actions are distinguished
According to the Strands that spring from their innate nature.

42. Calm, (self-)control, austerities, purity,
Patience, and uprightness,
Theoretical and practical knowledge, and religious faith,
Are the natural-born actions of brahmans.

43. Heroism, majesty, firmness, skill,
And not fleeing in battle also,
Generosity, and lordly nature,
Are the natural-born actions of warriors.

44. Agriculture, cattle-tending, and commerce
Are the natural-born actions of artisans;
Action that consists of service
Is likewise natural-born to a serf.

45. Taking delight in his own special kind of action,
A man attains perfection;
Delighting in one's own special action, success
How one reaches, that hear!

46. Whence comes the activity[7] of beings,
By whom this all is pervaded, —
Him worshiping by (doing) one's own appropriate action,
A man attains perfection.

47. Better one's own duty, (even) imperfect,
Than another's duty well performed.
Action pertaining to his own estate
Performing, he incurs no guilt.

48. Natural-born action, son of Kuntī,
Even tho it be faulty, one should not abandon.
For all undertakings by faults
Are dimmed, as fire by smoke.

49. His mentality unattached to any object,
Self-conquered, free from longings,
To the supreme perfection of actionlessness
He comes thru renunciation.

50. Having attained perfection, how to Brahman
He also attains, hear from Me,
In only brief compass, son of Kuntī;
Which is the highest culmination of knowledge.

51. With purified mentality disciplined,
And restraining himself with firmness,
Abandoning the objects of sense, sounds and the rest,
And putting away desire and loathing,

52. Cultivating solitude, eating lightly,
Restraining speech, body, and mind,
Devoted to the discipline of meditation constantly,
Taking refuge in dispassion,

53. From egotism, force, pride,
Desire, wrath, and possession
Freed, unselfish, calmed,
He is fit for becoming Brahman.

54. Having become Brahman, serene-souled,
He neither grieves nor longs;
Alike to all beings,
He attains supreme devotion to Me.

55. Thru devotion he comes to know Me,
What My measure is, and who I am, in very truth;
Then, knowing Me in very truth,
He enters into (Me) straightway.

56. Even tho all actions ever
He performs, relying on Me,
By My grace he reaches
The eternal, undying station.

57. With thy thoughts all actions
Casting upon Me,[8] devoted to Me,
Turning to discipline of mentality,
Keep thy mind ever fixed on Me.

58. If thy mind is on Me, all difficulties
Shalt thou cross over by My grace;
But if thru egotism thou
Wilt not heed, thou shalt perish.

59. If clinging to egotism
Thou thinkest 'I will not fight!,'
Vain is this thy resolve;
(Thine own) material nature will coerce thee.

60. Son of Kuntī, by thine own natural
Action held fast,
What thru delusion thou seekest not to do,
That thou shalt do even against thy will.

61. Of all beings, the Lord
In the heart abides, Arjuna,
Causing all beings to turn around
(As if) fixed in a machine,[9] by his magic power.

62. To Him alone go for refuge
With thy whole being, son of Bharata;
By His grace, supreme peace
And the eternal station shalt thou attain.

63. Thus to thee has been expounded the knowledge
That is more secret than the secret, by Me;
After pondering on it fully,
Act as thou thinkest best.

64. Further, the highest secret of all,
My supreme message, hear.
Because thou art greatly loved of Me,
Therefore I shall tell thee what is good for thee.

65. Be Me-minded, devoted to Me;
Worshiping Me, revere Me;
And to Me alone shalt thou go; truly to thee
I promise it — (because) thou art dear to Me.

66. Abandoning all (other) duties,
Go to Me as thy sole refuge;
From all evils I thee
Shall rescue: be not grieved!

67. This on thy part to no one not endowed with austerity,
Nor ever to one not devoted,
Nor to one not obedient, must be told,
Nor to one who murmurs against Me.

68. Whoso this supreme secret
Shall make known to My devotees,
Showing utmost devotion to Me,
Shall go just to Me, without a doubt.

69. And not than he among men
Is there any who does things more pleasing to Me;
Nor shall there be than he to Me
Any other dearer on earth.

70. And whoso shall study this
Colloquy on duty between us two,
By him with knowledge-worship I
Would be worshiped: so I hold.

71. With faith, and not murmuring against it,
What man even hears it,
He too shall be released, and the fair worlds
Of men of virtuous deeds shall he attain.

72. Has this been heard, son of Pṛthā,
By thee with concentrated thought?
Has the confusion of ignorance
In thee been destroyed, Dhanaṃjaya?

Arjuna said:

73. Destroyed the confusion; attention (to the truth) is won,
By Thy grace, on my part, O Changeless One;
I stand firm, with doubts dispersed;
I shall do Thy word.

Saṃjaya said:

74. Thus I of Vāsudeva
And the exalted son of Pṛthā
This colloquy have heard,
Marvelous and thrilling.

75. By the grace of Vyāsa have I heard
This supreme secret,
This discipline, from Kṛṣṇa the Lord of Discipline,
Speaking it Himself in very person.

76. O king, as I recall again and again
This marvelous colloquy,
And holy, of Keśava and Arjuna,
I thrill with joy at every moment.

77. And as I recall again and again that
Most wondrous form of Hari,
Great is my amazement, O king,
And I thrill with joy again and again.

78. Where is Kṛṣṇa the Lord of Discipline,
And where is the Bowman, the son of Pṛthā,
There fortune, victory, prosperity,
And statecraft are firmly fixed, I ween.

Here ends the Eighteenth Chapter, called Discipline of Renunciation unto Salvation.

THE END OF THE BHAGAVAD GĪTĀ.

NOTES TO THE TRANSLATION

Ś denotes the Sanskrit commentary of Śamkara; R, that of Rāmānuja.

Notes on Chapter I (pp. 3–8)

1. (Verse 10) Bhīṣma was the commander of the Kuru army. Bhīma, the third of the sons of Pāṇḍu, was not the actual leader of their army; he is here opposed to Bhīṣma for the sake of the word-play on the two names.
2. (Colophon) The titles given to each of the eighteen chapters in the final colophons are late additions, not parts of the original text. Many of them vary in the MSS. and printed texts, but it is hardly worth while to record these variations.

Notes on Chapter II (pp. 9–17)

1. (Vs 5) I.e., without waiting for such a punshiment in a future life. Interference with a guru's desires is a heinous sin. This verse has caused much unnecessary discussion; see *JAOS*. 52. 71 f.

2. (Vs 11) The meaning is that Arjuna shows ignorant presumption in daring to discuss learned topics while showing himself so uninformed as to mourn the dead. So essentially R. See *JAOS*. 52. 70 f.; and cf. *prājñavādikaḥ,* "talking as (pretending to be) wise," Mbh. ii. 2288 (Critical edition ii. 61. 38).

3. (Vs 14) So Garbe and Deussen; cf. Bṛhad Āraṇyaka Upaniṣad 4. 3. 10. S, 'senses,' or (alternatively) 'objects of sense'; R the latter; both supported only by fantastic etymologies. Hill follows the second, Telang and Barnett the first, of Ś's guesses.

4. (Vs 15) So Ś, Telang, Garbe, Deussen, Barnett; or, 'steadfast' (R, Senart. Hill).

5. (Vs 20) So, essentially, R, Telang, Barnett. The text reads: *nā'yam bhūtvā bhavitā vā na bhūyaḥ.* The second *na* is to be taken closely with *bhavitā* (together, 'will come not to be') which compound expression is negated by the first *na,* as in vs 12 *na . . . nāsam.* Otherwise, but implausibly, Ś (who understands *abhavitā*), and other moderns. The objection commonly raised to R's interpretation is that the soul should not be spoken of as having 'come to be,' since it has existed from everlasting. But this is a slight and superficial inconsistency, really only verbal in character; much more serious ones are very common in the Gītā.

6. (Vs 39) *Sāṃkhya:* see pp. 165 ff.

7. (Vs 42) Or, 'in talk about the Vedas'?

8. (Vs 43) So Ś, Telang, Garbe, Deussen, Barnett, Senart, Hill. A possible alternative would be 'rebirth and the fruit of actions.'

9. (Vs 45) *Sattva:* both Ś and R, followed by Barnett, take it to mean the 'Strand' (*guna*) of that name. This may be right, though seemingly inconsistent with the context. But *sattva* may also mean 'truth, reality' (so Deussen. Hill), 'purity,' or 'courage' (so Telang, Garbe).

10. (Vs 59) *Viṣayā vinivartante / nirāhārasya dehinaḥ / rasavarjam raso 'py asya / paraṃ dṛṣṭvā nivartate:* the fasting man, until he 'sees the highest,' cannot help feeling longing for food, i.e., for 'flavor,' the object of the sense of taste, though he feels no longing for the objects of the other senses. After a sufficiently long fast (interpreted as a sign that he 'sees the highest'), a man ceases even to feel hungry. Hindu commentators and modern interpreters have a different interpretation, abandoning the simple and familiar meaning of the word *rasa* (which can hardly mean anything but 'flavor' in the above sense, coming immediately after *viṣayāḥ* and clearly meant as one of the 'objects of sense'), for a more forced one.

11. (Vs 66) *Bhāvanā:* here, 'effective religious impulse'; the word *bhāvanā* means 'bringing to be, tendency to produce something (here, religious effort).' It is a technical word of the Mīmāmsā system. See Edgerton, *The Mīmāṅsā Nyāya Prakāsa,* Glossarial Index s.v., and p. 5 ff.

12. (Vs 70) Or, 'stability.'

13. (Vs 72) I.e., fixation in or of Brahman, or resulting in the attainment of Brahman. Ś, *brahmaṇi bhavā;* R, *brahmaprāpikā.*

14. (Vs 72) I.e., *nirvāṇa* in, or that is, Brahman; R, *nirvāṇamayaṃ brahma.*

Notes on Chapter III (pp. 18–22)

1. (Vs 2) *Vyāmiśrene 'va.* R reads *vyāmiśrenai 'va,* 'that are quite confused.' Cf. *JAOS.* 52. 73.

2. (Vs 3) *Sāṃkhya:* see ii. 39 and note.

3. (Vs 15) In xiv. 3, 4 Brahman clearly equals Prakṛti (cf. p. 154); and here also, in the first two occurrences at least, it is probably felt vaguely in some such way (cf. the notes of Garbe and Hill). But the whole progression of terms in vss 14. 15 cannot be forced into a really logical sequence; however the words be interpreted, the conclusion does not follow from the premises. 'Worship' is not the starting-point of the series but an intermediate term.

4. (Vs 16) *Aghāyur:* taken by Ś, R, and some moderns as a compound of *agha* and *āyus,* 'of evil life.' It seems to occur only here in classical Sanskrit; but it is probably to be understood as the Vedic *aghāya.* not a compound but from a denominative verb stem based on *agha.*

5. (Vs 30) *Saṃnyasya:* see note on v. 10, below.

6. (Vs 38) So R, Barnett, Deussen, Senart, Hill (also Schlegel and Boehtlingk); according to Ś. Telang, Garbe, 'this [knowledge].'

7. (Vs 41) *Jñāna* and *vijñāna:* see Edgerton in *Festschrift M. Winternitz* (Leipzig, 1933), pp. 217–220.

Notes on Chapter IV (pp. 23–27)

1. (Vs 25) Ritualists.

2. (Vs 25) Philosophical mystics; the following is a cryptically figurative way of saying that they abandon ritual action and devote their thoughts to the Brahman alone.

3. (Vs 26) Ascetics who seek to annihilate all the senses.

4. (Vs 26) Men of 'discipline' or disinterested activity, who allow the senses to act on the objects of sense but without attachment to the latter.

5. (Vs 27) Followers of the *'Sāṃkhya'* way of knowledge with complete renunciation of action.

6. (Vs 29) Those who pursue the method of breath-exercises, as in the (later) Yoga.

7. (Vs 30) Those who (like many Jains) seek salvation by suicide, through slow starvation.

8. (Vs 32) Or, 'performed, carried out.'

9. (Vs 32) Or, 'mouth'; so Garbe and Senart, who understand 'are offered to Brahman'; it may, however, mean only 'are performed before Brahman.' This, to be sure, perhaps comes to the same thing, but is less definite, and perhaps purposely so. Some moderns follow Ś in understanding the Veda as meant, which to me is most implausible. Another possibility is that *brahmaṇo mukhe* means 'in the fire (of sacrifice),' as that by which the gods eat the offerings.

Notes on Chapter V (pp. 28–31)

1. (Vs 4) For *sāṃkhya* (reason-method) see ii. 39 and note.

2. (Vs 10) *Brahmany ādhāya karmāni: ādhāya* here must mean the same as *saṃnyasya* iii. 30, xii. 6, and xviii. 57. Ś and some moderns understand 'doing all as acts of devotion to Brahman' (or 'to Me,' iii. 30 and xviii. 57). Others, essentially with R, 'realizing that it is Brahman (or God) that does all acts and that the individual is not the doer.' If the latter is right, as I think likely though not certain, it is not necessary to take Brahman here as equal to Prakṛti, with R and Hill (though this is in itself quite possible, cf. note on iii. 15). Since Brahman or God is all, all acts must really be done by Him; and this despite the fact that elsewhere we are told often and clearly enough that all actions are done by Prakṛti. Cf. p. 147 f.

3. (Vs 10) The same figure in Buddhistic Sanskrit, *Daśabhūmika Sūtra* V, *gāthā* 29 (ed. Rahder and Susa, 1931). It is a very effective image to one who

has seen lotus-covered Indian ponds. Drops of water stand away from the leaves as if from an oiled surface.

4. (Vs 27) *Nāsābhyantaracāriṇau:* i.e., as the breath collectively passes. Though *prāṇa* properly means the breath above the diaphragm and *apāna* the breath below it, they are frequently used together to denote the vital breath as a whole; and even more commonly *prāṇa* alone is so used. The common renderings 'expiration' and 'inspiration,' for *prāṇā* and *apāna,* or vice versa, are groundless; significantly, those who hold to them have never been able to agree as to which was which. See G. W. Brown, *JAOS.* 39. 104–112.

Notes on Chapter VI (pp. 32–37)

1. (Vs 8) *Jñānavijñāna:* see note on iii. 41.

2. (Vs 8) The precise interpretation of *kūṭastha* is not entirely clear, and the commentators had no consistent and reliable tradition (cf. note on xii. 3). S glosses the word by *aprakampya* ('unshaking, unwavering'). In Pāli we find the same word as *kūṭattha,* and certainly it means something like 'not subject to change'; perhaps literally 'abiding on a mountaintop,' as if 'above the battle,' not subject to external influences. So apparently Barnett ('set on high').

3. (Vs 13) That is, 'straight, stiff.'

4. (Vs 26) So Ś, R; most moderns, 'to whatever object,' despite the ablative form (*yato-yato,* which might perhaps be due to attraction to the correlative, *tatas tato*). Yet the grammatically stricter interpretation of Ś, R seems possible, at least.

5. (Vs 28) This is generally taken as an epithet of 'bliss': 'to endless bliss which involves contact with Brahman.' This is possible, but not necessary.

6. (Vs 29) *Ātmānaṃ:* Himself. So Garbe and Deussen with both Ś and R, *svātman* or *svam ātmānam.* Surely not 'Self' abstractly (Barnett, Hill) or *'l'ātman'* (Senart).

7. (Vs 32) I.e., who sees that pleasure and pain to others are the same as to himself.

8. (Vs 33) *Sāmya:* 'sameness,' 'non-difference,' and also 'indifference,' 'treating as alike.'

9. (Vs 39) *Etan me saṃsayaṃ kṛṣṇa:* reading *etan;* R, *etam,* 'this my doubt.'

Notes on Chapter VII (pp. 38–41)

1. (Vs 2) *Jñānaṃ te 'haṃ savijñānam:* see note on iii. 41.

2. (Vs 6) Both Ś and R, followed by Telang, Garbe, Deussen. Barnett, and Hill, take this to refer to both the 'natures' of vss 4 and 5. This is verbally pos-

sible, and certainly better than Senart's interpretation, which refers it to the 'lower' nature alone. If to either, the pronoun must refer rather to the last mentioned ('higher') nature; so I understand it. This may be philosophically less reasonable; but the Gītā is not a metaphysical treatise. As the following verses show, the author is thinking primarily of God's supreme essence.

3. (Vs 16) Or, 'wealth,' with Ś, Telang, Garbe, Deussen, Barnett, Senart, Hill. But R *aiśvarya.* With this verse cf. Mbh. 12. 342. 33 ff., which also mentions four classes of devotees (*bhakta*), the highest of which consists of those who are exclusive worshipers (*ekāntinaḥ* . . . *ananyadevatāḥ*). The other three are unfortunately not named, but are all stigmatized as *phalakāma.*

4. (Vs 22) Construe with R and Garbe (see the latter's note).

5. (Vs 24) 'Fools' take the external manifestation of Kṛṣṇa to be all there is to Kṛṣṇa. Whether they think him a man or a 'god,' they are equally in error; the author does not distinguish between these two possible errors.

6. (Vs 29) On the terms used in this and the next verse see vss 3 and 4 in the next chapter, with notes.

Notes on Chapter VIII (pp. 42–45)

1. (Vs 3) Here the individual soul as distinguished from the universal soul and from matter.

2. (Vs 3) 'Karma,' man's own action, which causes him to be reborn in this or that condition in future births.

3. (Vs 4) Virtually *prakṛti,* 'material nature.'

4. (Vs 4) All the terms used here are somewhat loose and vague; the language is grandiloquent.

5. (Vs 4) Viṣṇu is identified with *yajña,* 'sacrifice, worship,' in a standard way in the Brāhmaṇas. See Garbe's note.

6. (Vs 21) Or, 'light'; R mentions this as an alternative.

7. (Vs 23) On this and the following verses, in which an Upaniṣad notion (BṛhU. 6. 2. 15 f., ChU. 5. 10. 1 ff.) is misinterpreted or reinterpreted by the Gītā, see Edgerton, 'The Hour of Death,' *Annals Bhandarkar Institute,* 8. 219–249, especially 245 ff.

Notes on Chapter IX (pp. 46–49)

1. (Vs 1) *Jñānaṃ vijñānasahitaṃ:* See note on iii. 41.

2. (Vs 26) Or perhaps, 'from him that has given himself.'

3. (Vs 28) *Saṃnyāsayoga:* Ś and R take the compound word as a unitary concept. This is quite possible, and in my opinion probable, in spite of v. 1 ff., which

distinguish *saṃnyāsa* and *yoga* (for which reason most moderns understand here 'in renunciation and [or] discipline [of action]'). 'Renunciation' is also a *yoga,* 'discipline,' in a more general sense; cf. iii. 3. The yoga of v. 1 is short for the specific *karmayoga* of iii. 3 etc., which is used in the following verse v. 2.

Notes on Chapter X (pp. 50–54)

1. (Vs 6) With Garbe I take this to imply that the human race is founded by a Manu at the beginning of each of the four world-ages (*yuga*). The theory of 7, or 14, Manus is rather late and cannot be proved to have existed as early as the Gītā; but even if it did, the thought of the four world-ages easily suggests four Manus also. Rigid consistency is not to be expected here.

2. (Vs 6) So rightly Senart; *bhāva,* 'coming to be, origination,' as in ii. 16.

3. (Vs 7) *Vibhūti:* R, *vibhūtir aiśvaryam . . . madāyattopattisthitipravṛttirūpām vibhūtim.* Ś, *vistāram;* Anandagiri on Ś here, *vividhā bhūtir bhavanaṃ vaibhavaṃ sarvātmakatvaṃ.* Both meanings, 'lordship, power' (cf. Kathāsaritsāgara 17. 138, *prabhūṇām hi vibhūtyandhā . . . matiḥ,* 'the mind of the lords, blinded by power' or 'greatness'), and 'varied manifestation', are contained in the word. I have tried to suggest both by the term 'supernal manifestation.' Deussen, *Machtentfaltung,* which is very apt. The word occurs repeatedly in this chapter (vss 7, 16, 18, 19, 40, 41) and is chosen as the title of the chapter in the colophon.

4. (Vs 8) So R.

5. (Vs 12) Or, 'light'; so Ś, R.

6. (Vs 12) Or, 'unborn and supernally-manifested' (*vibhu,* related to *vibhūti,* see note on vs 7); so Ś and most moderns; R ignores the word. The commonest meaning of *vibhu,* however, is simply 'lord'; for this reason I have so rendered it.

7. (Vs 13) Probably Asita Devala is one person, rather than two; the epic knows such a personage.

8. (Vs 19) Or, 'divine, supernatural.' For this line R reads *vibhūtīr ātmanaḥ śubhāḥ,* 'my fair supernal-manifestations.'

9. (Vs 29) *Saṃyamatām,* with etymological word-play on Yama (whose name is originally not connected with this root, but came to be felt as connected).

10. (Vs 30) Ś 'reckoners.' The root *kal-* is used with intent to play on Kāla, 'time.' The correct interpretation is given by P. E. Dumont in his note on Īśvaragītā 7. 16 (see his edition of that work, Baltimore, 1933), where this line is repeated.

11. (Vs 30) Ś 'lion or tiger'; R ignores the word; Veṅkaṭanātha, a subcommentator on R, says 'lion.'

12. (Vs 32) Of them that speak: *pravadatām* can only be personal, and is therefore not partitive genitive but possessive. R and (alternatively) Ś, followed by many moderns, would make it refer to various kinds of argument (as apartitive genitive), which seems to me a grammatical impossibility.

13. (Vs 34) All these words are grammatically feminine in Sanskrit.

14. (Vs 36) *Sattvaṃ sattvavatāṃ aham: sattva* has many meanings, among them 'courage.' But *sattvavant* is regularly used only in the sense of 'courageeous.' This interpretation accords with the rest of the verse, which clearly deals with warlike and royal matters, which to the Hindus are identical (the warrior caste, *kṣatriya,* is the same as the royal caste, *rājanya*). Even gambling belongs specifically to this social group. I think that R meant 'courage' by his gloss, *mahāmanastvam;* and Ś may well have had the same idea (all he says is *sattvavatāṃ sāttvikānām*). The subcommentaries of Veṅkaṭanātha and Ānandagiri, wrongly as I think, understand 'goodness of the good'; and so most moderns.

15. (Vs 41) Or, 'lordliness, power'; see note on vs 7.

Notes on Chapter XI (pp. 55–61)

1. (Vs 18) So Ś, R, and most moderns. Less likely, 'treasure-store.'

2. (Vs 19) Or, 'mouth.'

3. (Vs 21) So, literally, Ś, Telang. Deussen, Senart; R, followed by Garbe, Barnett, Hill, 'draw near unto Thee.'

4. (Vs 26) The word 'enter' is in the author's mind; when, in the next verse, he comes to use it, he makes the goal more specific: 'thy mouths.'

5. (Vs 29) Or, 'people'; so most commentators and interpreters, here and in vss 30, 32.

6. (Vs 37) So taken by most moderns; Ś and R, followed by Barnett, translate this phrase as 'first creator even of Brahman (masculine).'

7. (Vs 38) Less likely, 'treasure-store.'

8. (Vs 40) *Anantavīryāmitavikramas tvaṃ: anatavīrya* seems to me better taken with R as a separate vocative; most interpreters follow Ś in taking it as a part of the following compound.

Notes on Chapter XII (pp. 62–64)

1. (Vs 3) Immovable (*kūṭastha*)*:* see note on vi. 8. Here Ś (departing from his previous explanation) understands abiding in trickery,' i.e., in *māyā,* the world-illusion of which God is the 'overseer.' This is worth quoting as an instance of the absurdity and inconsistency of which even the greatest commentators are

sometimes guilty. He adds, to be sure, an alternative interpretation, which is substantially that adopted here.

2. (Vs 4) Either 'to all experiences,' indifferent to the results, as in ii. 48 etc. (so Ś, Deussen, Senart), or 'to all beings,' as in vi. 9 etc. (so, essentially, R and Garbe); or—very likely—both may be more or less implied.

3. (Vs 20) Cf. x. 18. According to Ś, followed by Telang, Garbe, Barnett, Hill, '(means of attaining) immortality.'

Notes on Chapter XIII (pp. 65–68)

1. (Vs 4) So Ś, R. It is implausible to suppose with Garbe that the Upaniṣads would be called *chandas.*

2. (Vs 4) So Ś, who quotes from BṛhU. 1. 4. 7 as an example. R refers the word to Bādarāyaṇa's Vendānta Sūtras, and is followed by Garbe, Barnett, and others. I consider it very improbable that this work existed in the time of the Gītā. And if *chandas* means the Vedic hymns, the Upaniṣads would not otherwise be mentioned in this verse. See *JAOS*. 52. 74.

3. (Vs 6) I.e., of senses with sense-objects? See Hill's note, which I endorse. The usual rendering is something like 'aggregation (of corporeal elements),' which is out of place here in a list of qualities, not physical elements. R has a different but very forced interpretation.

4. (Vs 11) Viz. salvation (Ś).

5. (Vs 12) *Anādi matparaṃ brahma:* so R (*anādi matparam*); Ś divides *anādimat paraṃ,* 'the beginningless supreme Brahman,' and modern translators generally follow him. The introduction of 'Me' as the basis of the impersonal Brahman naturally offends those who seek systematic consistency in the Gītā; but xiv. 27 proves that *matparam* is quite possible. Yet the rival interpretation is also possible.

6. (Vs 13) Or, 'mouths.'

7. (Vs 13) Or perhaps, 'ears'; so Telang, Garbe, Senart; but Ś, R, Deussen, Barnett, Hill, 'faculty of hearing,' which is more in accord with general usage.

8. (Vs 14) So Ś, Barnett, Hill; otherwise R, Telang, Garbe, Deussen, Senart.

9. (Vs 17) *Jyotiṣām api taj jyotis.* According to Ś, R, and most moderns this means that it is the illuminating power of all lights (sun, etc.). This is possible, but *jyotiṣām* may also, and in my opinion more probably, be partitive; cf. Chapter x, passim.) 'Among lights it is that light which is beyond darkness.'

10. (Vs 17) So Ś, Telang, Garbe, Deussen, Barnett. 'The goal of knowledge' (salvation) is distinguished from the 'object of knowledge' (here, the thing known).

11. (Vs 17) *Dhiṣṭitam:* the v. l. *viṣṭhitam,* 'fixed variously,' is read for *dhiṣṭhitam* by both Ś and R; nevertheless it is probably a *lectio facilior* (as such it is a common substitute for *dhiṣṭhita-* in the epic).

12. (Vs 18) So Ś; R, 'is fitted for.'

13. (Vs 20) *Kāryakaraṇakartṛtve:* Ś, R explain *kārya* as 'elemental body,' which is an 'effect' in the later Sāṃkhya sense, and *karaṇa* (R *kāraṇa*) as the senses with *manas* (and *ahaṃkāra* and *buddhi,* Ś), which are 'causes' or 'factors' (productive elements) in that same sense. These both are construed as depending on *kartṛtve,* 'in the production of effects and causes,' i.e., of gross body and senses. Approximately so most moderns (Telang, Garbe, Senart, Hill, and apparently Barnett). I find this very forced and artificial. The only natural interpretation is to take *kārya-karaṇakartṛ* as a three-member dvandva, made into an abstract by adding the suffix *-tva.* The three nouns derived from the root *kṛ,* 'act,' are meant to include all phases of action (cf. xviii. 18 for a very close parallel, where *karman* replaces *kārya*): *kārya,* 'thing to be done'; *karaṇa,* 'means of doing it'; *kartṛ,* 'doer, agent'; the addition of *-tva* makes the whole compound mean approximately 'effectuation, instrumentality, and agency.' *Prakṛti* alone is at the bottom of all that concerns all of these, that is, all phases of action. So in xviii. 18 *karaṇa, karman, and kartṛ* constitute the threefold 'complete summary' of action. Deussen comes very close to this, but wrongly takes *-tva* only with *kartr.*

14. (Vs 23) Telang and Garbe understand this to mean 'whatever his moral conduct may be'; which introduces an idea not suggested in the Sanskrit. Rather, with R, whatever stage of transmigration he may be in.

15. (Vs 24) *'Sāṃkhya:* see ii. 39. note.

16. (Vs 25) Devoted to the holy revelation (*Śrutiparāyaṇāḥ*)*:* so Deussen. *Śruti* usually suggests this; possibly, however, it may mean only 'to what they hear'; so most interpreters.

17. (Vs 28) Since the same Lord (= soul, cf. v. 15) is in all beings, the self of others is one's own self, and if he injures others, he injures himself. That this is the meaning seems obvious to me; but for some reason, it has escaped all commentators and modern interpreters examined by me except Deussen (and possibly Barnett, whose rendering is obscure to me).

Notes on Chapter XIV (pp. 69–72)

1. (Vs 20) That spring from the body (*dehasamudbhavān*)*:* so Hill; and R *dehākārapariṇataprakṛtisamudbhavān.* Ś, followed by Telang, Garbe, Deussen, Barnett. Senart, 'from which the body arises.'

2. (Vs 22) As both Ś and R point out, these are the essential characteristics of the three 'Strands' of nature, 'goodness, passion, and darkness' respectively.

3. (Vs 24) So Ś, R, and most moderns; but it may equally well mean 'steadfast' (so Deussen, Senart).

Notes on Chapter XV (pp. 73–75)

1. (Vs 1) Not (as has often been wrongly suggested) the banyan, which drops runners from its branches to form new roots. As Hill points out, this is not true of the peepal. Hill ingeniously tries to show that the metaphor nevertheless fits the peepal. I think it is unnecessary to do this; the author may well have meant his statement as a deliberate paradox, not intending to suggest that the actual tree has 'roots aloft and branches below.' The choice of the peepal, rather than any other tree, to symbolize material existence, was then dictated not by its specific nature, but by the fact that it is a well known and venerated tree. That the author himself erroneously confused the banyan and the peepal trees, as suggested by Deussen, seems absurd; both trees are too familiar in Indian life. The figure is taken from Katha Up. 6. 1, where in the next verse it is described as 'a great terror, an uplifted thunderbolt' (appropriate terms for the *saṃsāra*). That it means also the 'soul' (v. Schroeder, *Festschrift E. Kuhn,* 59 ff.) seems grotesquely impossible.

2. (Vs 6) Or, 'light' (so R).

3. (Vs 8) *Īśvara:* here 'individual soul.' Not 'lord of the senses' (R), nor 'lord of the body and other material elements' (Ś).

4. (Vs 9) Or, 'resorting to,' cf. iv. 6; more literally, 'presiding over' or 'taking his stand upon.'

5. (Vs 16) *Kūṭastha:* see note on vi. 8. xii. 3.

Notes on Chapter XVI (pp .76–78)

1. (Vs 2) Or, 'liberality.' Ś, 'renunciation, because generosity has been mentioned (in vs 1)'; most interpreters follow him. But his reason is not conclusive; such lists often contain duplications. And R says 'liberality.'

2. (Vs 7) I.e., what should or should not be done; cf. xviii. 30. So Telang, Deussen. The expressions are very general; Ś, R, and most moderns are too specific.

3. (Vs 17) So Ś; R, 'of the arrogance of wealth and pride,' which is implausible (cf. vs 10).

4. (Vs 19) *Saṃsāreṣu narādhamān / kṣipāmy:* Garbe and Senart take *saṃsāreṣu* closely with *narādhamān:* 'the lowest men in the round of existences.' This misses the point; *saṃsāreṣu* clearly goes with *kṣipāmi.*

Notes on Chapter XVII (pp. 79–82)

1. (Vs 5) So Garbe, Deussen, Senart (and Telang, but with 'stubbornness' for 'violence'); Ś, Barnett, Hill, 'with the power of desire and passion'; R does not explain the word.

2. (Vs 23) R says *brahman* here means the Veda. In a sense he is right; but this hardly tells the whole story. The Veda is conceived as the mystic verbal expression of the Absolute, the one universal power. Hill's summary, p. 93, is excellent. Verse 24 refers to ritualists, 25 to followers of the 'way of knowledge,' 26 and 27 to followers of 'practical' methods. *Om* is the ritualistic sacred syllable; *tat* suggests the mystic, magic monism of the Upaniṣads (*tat tvam asi,* etc.); *sat* is sufficiently explained in vs 26.

Notes on Chapter XVIII (pp. 83–91)

1. (Vs 13) *Sāṃkhya:* see ii. 39 and note.

2. (Vs 14) Much needless trouble has been caused by this verse, owing to attempts to make it too philosophical, and particularly to make it fit the theories of the later so-called Sāṃkhya system. It is a quite simple and naive attempt to suggest the factors which are involved in carrying out any action whatever; it is fundamentally wrong to try to identify each 'factor' with bodily parts or 'Sāṃkhya' *tattvas.* Each of the five words is to be taken in the simplest possible sense, and no comment is really needed—except that all existing comments are worthless and misleading.

3. (Vs 18) Cf. xiii. 20, where the three elements are *kārya, karaṇa,* and *kartṛ.* Here *kārya* is (rather poorly) replaced by *karman.*

4. (Vs 19) Not 'the Sāṃkhya system' (Ś, Telang, Garbe).

5. (Vs 22) Or, 'with true reason.'

6. (Vs 37) So Deussen; or, 'of one's own intelligence' (so Ś, first rendering, and Barnett, Hill). R, and alternatively Ś, followed by Telang, Garbe, Senart. 'from clarity of knowledge of the self.'

7. (Vs 46) Or, 'origin.'

8. (Vs 57) See note on v. 10.

9. (Vs 61) As puppets in a puppet-play, according to Ś's plausible suggestion.

INTERPRETATION OF THE BHAGAVAD GĪTĀ

FIRST PART

PRELIMINARY CHAPTERS

CHAPTER I

Introductory

To most good Vishnuites, and indeed to most Hindus, the Bhagavad Gītā is what the New Testament is to good Christians. It is their chief devotional book. In it many millions of Indians have for centuries found their principal source of religious inspiration.

In form, it consists mainly of a long dialog, which is almost a monolog. The principal speaker is Kṛṣṇa, who in his human aspect is merely one of the secondary heroes of the Mahābhārata, the great Hindu epic. But, according to the Gītā itself, he is in truth a manifestation of the Supreme Deity in human form. Hence the name — the Song (*gītā*) of the Blessed One or the Lord (*Bhagavad*).[1] The other speaker in the dialog is Arjuna, one of the five sons of Pāṇḍu who are the principal heroes of the Mahābhārata. The conversation between Arjuna and Kṛṣṇa is supposed to take place just before the battle which is the main theme of the great epic. Kṛṣṇa is acting as Arjuna's charioteer. Arjuna sees in the ranks of the opposing army a large number of his own kinsmen and intimate friends. He is horror-stricken at the thought of fighting against them, and forthwith lays down his weapons, saying he would rather be killed than kill them. Kṛṣṇa replies, justifying the fight on various grounds, the chief of which is that man's real self or soul is immortal and independent of the body; it "neither kills nor is killed"; it has no part in either the actions or the sufferings of the body. In response to further questions by Arjuna, he gradually develops views of life and destiny as a whole, which it is the purpose of this book to explain. In the course of the exposition he declares himself to be the Supreme Godhead, and reveals to Arjuna, as a special act of grace, a vision of his mystic supernal form. All this apparently goes on while the two armies stand drawn up in battle array, waiting to attack each other. This dramatic absurdity need not concern us seriously. It is likely that the Bhagavad Gītā was not a part of the original epic narrative. Possibly it was composed, or inserted in its present position, by a later interpolator.[2] To be sure, he must have had in

[1] More fully and exactly, the title of the work is "the mystic doctrines (*upaniṣad*) sung (or proclaimed) by the Blessed One."

[2] Such interpolations are numerous in the Mahābhārata; so numerous that we may fairly regard them as a regular habit. The great epic early attained such prestige among the Hindus that later authors were eager to win immortality for their works by framing them in so distinguished a setting. If the author of the Bhagavad Gītā used an older work to frame his own, he merely followed a custom which was not only common, but seemed

mind the dramatic situation in which he has placed the Gītā, for he repeatedly makes reference to it. But these references are purely formal and external; they do not concern the essentials of the work. We must think of the Gītā primarily as a unit, complete in itself, without reference to its surroundings. Its author, or whoever placed it in its present position, was interested chiefly in the religious doctrines to be set forth, not in external dramatic forms.

This is not to say that the author was lacking in artistic power. He was, on the contrary, a poet of no mean capacity. Indeed, we must think of his work as a poem: a religious, devotional poem. Its appeal is to the emotions rather than to the intellect. It follows that in order to understand the Gītā one must have a certain capacity for understanding its poetic, emotional point of view. One must be able and willing to adopt the poet's attitude: to feel with him. I say, to feel with him: not necessarily to think with him. It is possible to understand and enjoy sympathetically a poetic expression of an emotional attitude without sharing the poet's intellectual opinions. Philosophically speaking, the attitude of the Gītā is mystical. A mystic would probably prefer to say that it appeals to the mystic intuition, rather than to the emotions, as I put it. That is a question of terms, or perhaps better of philosophic outlook. My mystic critic would at any rate agree that it does not appeal to the reasoning faculty of mankind. The "opinions" which it presupposes or sets forth are not so much "opinions" in the intellectual sense as emotional — or, let us say if you like, intuitional — points of view. They are not supported by logic; they are simply proclaimed, as immediately perceived by the soul, or revealed by the grace of God. It is not my purpose to discuss their validity. That would indeed be futile. To the mystic they are above reason, to the rationalist below it; to both they are disconnected with it. Either you accept them immediately, without argument, or you do not. Argument will not move you in either case. But even a convinced rationalist, if he has some power of poetic appreciation, can follow much of the Gītā's presentation with sympathy, the sort of sympathy which would be inspired in him by any exalted poetry.

The poetic inspiration found in many of the Gītā's lines [3] can hardly be fully appreciated unless they are presented in a poetic form. We are fortunate in having a beautiful English rendering by Sir Edwin Arnold, from which those who cannot read Sanskrit may get, on the whole, a good idea of the living spirit of the poem. It takes a poet to reproduce poetry. Arnold was a poet, and a very gifted one. I am very glad to be able to re-

to the Hindu mind entirely natural and innocent. The Hindus of ancient times had little notion of what we consider the rights of authorship. To their minds any literary composition belonged to the world, not to its author.

[3] Not all of them; it must be confessed that the Gītā is sometimes commonplace.

produce his rendering in this volume. My own function is that of an analytic commentator; a more humble function, but one which has its uses, particularly in the case of a work that was produced in a place and at a time so remote from us.

This remoteness in time and scene makes exceptionally important one of the critic's duties: that of making clear the historical setting of his author. As every author, even the most inspired of poets and prophets, is a product of his environment, so we cannot understand the Bhagavad Gītā without knowing something of doctrines which flourished in its native land, during and before its time. It was composed in India, in Sanskrit, the ancient sacred and literary language of Brahmanic civilization. We do not know its author's name (indeed, almost all the early literature of India is anonymous). Nor can we date it with any accuracy; all that we can say is that it was probably composed before the beginning of our era, but not more than a few centuries before it. We do know this: it was preceded by a long literary and intellectual activity, covering perhaps a thousand years or even more, and reaching back to the hymns of the Rig Veda itself, the oldest monument of Hindu literature. And the Gītā's sayings are rooted in those of this older literature. It was born out of the same intellectual environment. It quotes from older works several stanzas and parts of stanzas. There are few important expressions found in the Gītā which cannot be paralleled from more ancient works. Its originality consists mainly in a difference of emphasis, in a fuller development of some inherited themes, and in some significant omissions of themes which were found in its predecessors.

It is equally true, tho less important for our purposes, that the Bhagavad Gītā itself has had an enormous influence on later Hindu religious literature. It has even had some influence on European and American literature of the last century, during which it became known to the western world. To mention one instance: a verse found in the Gītā was imitated by Emerson in the first verse of his poem on "Brahma":

If the red slayer think he slays,
  Or if the slain think he is slain,
They know not well the subtle ways
  I keep, and pass, and turn again.

Compare Bhagavad Gītā ii. 19:

Who believes him a slayer,
  And who thinks him slain,
Both these understand not:
  He slays not, is not slain.

To be sure, this stanza is not original with the Gītā; it is quoted from the Kaṭha Upaniṣad. It is more likely, however, that Emerson got it from the Gītā than from the less well-known Upaniṣad text. But the later influence of the Gītā lies outside the scope of this volume. I shall content myself with setting forth the doctrines of the Gītā and their origins.

Especially close is the connection between the Bhagavad Gītā and the class of works called Upaniṣads. These are the earliest extensive treatises dealing with philosophical subjects in India. About a dozen of them, at least, are older than the Gītā, whose author knew and quoted several. The Gītā itself is indeed regarded as an Upaniṣad (its manuscripts regularly call it so in their colophons), and has quite as good a right to the title as many later works that are so called.[4] All the works properly called Upaniṣads have this in common, that they contain mainly speculations on some or all of the following topics: the nature of the universe, its origin, purpose, and guiding principle; the nature of man, his physical and his "hyper-physical" constitution, his duty, his destiny, and his relation to the rest of the universe, particularly to the guiding principle thereof, whether treated personally or impersonally. Now, these are precisely the questions with which the Bhagavad Gītā is concerned. The answers attempted vary greatly, not only in different Upaniṣads, but often in adjoining parts of the same Upaniṣad. This also is true of the Gītā, and is eminently characteristic of the literature to which it and the Upaniṣads belong. We sometimes hear of a "system" of the Upaniṣads. In my opinion there is no such thing. Nor is there a "system" of thought in the Bhagavad Gītā, in the sense of a unitary, logically coherent, and exclusive structure of metaphysics. He who looks for such a thing in any work of this period will be disappointed. Or, worse yet, he may be tempted to apply Procrustean methods, and by excisions or strained interpretations to force into a unified mold the sayings of a writer who never dreamed of the necessity or desirability of such unity. The Upaniṣads and the Bhagavad Gītā contain starts toward various *systems*; but none of them contains a single *system*, except possibly in the sense that one trend may be more prominent than its rivals in an individual work or part of a work. Still less can we speak of a single system as taught by the Upaniṣads as a whole.

The very notion of a philosophic "system" did not exist in India in the time of the early Upaniṣads and the Gītā. In later times the Hindus produced various systems of philosophy, which are fairly comparable with what we are accustomed to understand by that term, despite a clearly professed practical purpose which we moderns do not usually associate with

[4] The word *upaniṣad* may be translated "secret, mystic doctrine"; it is a title that is often claimed by all sorts of works, some of which hardly deserve to be called philosophical in any sense.

"philosophy." These systems all grew, at least in large measure, out of the older speculations of the Upaniṣads. Each later thinker chose out of the richness of Upaniṣadic thought such elements as pleased him, and constructed his logically coherent system on that basis. Thus, the Upaniṣads, broadly speaking, are the prime source of all the rival philosophies of later India. But they themselves are more modest. They do not claim to have succeeded in bringing under one rubric the absolute and complete truth about man and the universe. If they seem at times to make such claims, these statements are to be understood as tentative, not final; and often they are contradicted by an adjoining passage in which a very different viewpoint finds expression. This may seem to us naive. But I think it would be truer, as well as more charitable, to regard it as a sign of intellectual modesty, combined with an honest and burning eagerness for truth, conceived as leading to man's mastery over his environment.

Thus there grew up in Upaniṣadic circles not one but a group of attempts to solve the "riddles of the universe." The Bhagavad Gītā, we have seen, belongs to these circles intellectually, and many of its favorite themes are derived from the older Upaniṣads. More important than this is the fact that it shares with them the trait of intellectual fluidity or tentativeness to which I have just referred. Unlike many later Hindu philosophic works, which also derive from the Upaniṣads but which select and systematize their materials, the Gītā is content to present various rival formulas, admitting at least a provisional validity to them all. To be sure, it has its favorites. But we can usually find in its own text expressions which, in strict logic, contradict its most cardinal doctrines. From the non-logical, mystical viewpoint of the Gītā this is no particular disadvantage. Rationalistic logic simply does not apply to its problems.

In one other respect there is an important difference of fundamental attitude between the Bhagavad Gītā and most western philosophic thought. All Hindu philosophy has a practical aim. It seeks the truth, but not the truth for its own sake. It is truth as a means of human salvation that is its object. In other words, all Hindu philosophy is religious in basis. To the Hindu mind, "the truth shall make you free." Otherwise there is no virtue in it. This is quite as true of the later systems as of the early and less systematic speculations. To all of them knowledge is a means to an end. This attitude has its roots in a still more primitive belief, which appears clearly in the beginnings of Vedic philosophy and is still very much alive in the early Upaniṣads: the belief in the magic power of knowledge. To the early Hindus, as to mankind in early stages of development the world over, "knowledge is power" in a very direct sense. Whatever you know you control, directly, and by virtue of your knowledge. The primitive magician gets his neighbors, animal, human, or supernatural, into his power, by acquiring knowledge of them. So the early Vedic thinkers sought to control the most fundamental and universal powers by *knowing* them. This belief the Hindus of classical times never quite outgrew. The Sanskrit word *vidyā*, "knowledge," means also "magic." Let westerners not be scornful of this. Down to quite modern times the same idea prevailed in Europe. In Shakespeare's *Tempest*, Prospero the scholar proves his learning by feats of magic; and in Robert Greene's play, *Friar Bacon and Friar Bungay*, Roger Bacon, the greatest of medieval English scholars, is represented as a mighty magician, and a contest of scholarship between him and a rival German scholar resolves itself into a mere test of their powers in necromancy. In short, knowledge meant primarily magic power, to the popular mind of that day. Even tho Greene doubtless intended his play as a farce, and did not take this notion seriously, still he would not have parodied the belief if it had not flourished in his time. As in Europe, so in India, the more advanced thinkers early began to keep their speculations free from magic, in its cruder forms. Even such a comparatively early work as the Bhagavad Gītā has no traces of the magical use of knowledge for the attainment of trivial, worldly ends, tho many such traces are still found in the Upaniṣads, its immediate predecessors. To this extent it marks an advance over them, and stands on essentially the same footing with the best of the later systematic philosophies. But the Bhagavad Gītā and the later systems agree with the early Upaniṣadic thinkers in their practical attitude towards speculation. They all seek the truth, not because of its abstract interest, but because in some sense or other they think that a realization of the truth about man's place in the universe and his destiny will solve all man's problems; free him from all the troubles of life; in short, bring him to the *summum bonum*, whatever they conceive that to be. Just as different thinkers differ as to what that truth is, so they also differ in their definitions of salvation or of the *summum bonum*, and of the best practical means of attaining it. Indeed, as we have seen, the early thinkers, including the author of the Gītā, frequently differ with themselves on such points. But they all agree in this fundamental attitude towards the objects of speculation. They are primarily religious rather than philosophical. And the historic origin of their attitude, in primitive notions about the magic power of knowledge, has left a trace which I think was never fully effaced, altho it was undoubtedly transcended and transfigured.

CHAPTER II

The Origins of Hindu Speculation

The records of Hindu religious thought, as of Hindu literature in general, begin with the Rig Veda. This is a collection consisting mostly of hymns of praise and prayer to a group of deities who are primarily personified powers of nature — sun, fire, wind, sky, and the like — with the addition of some gods whose original nature is obscure. The religion represented by the Rig Veda, however, is by no means a simple or primitive nature-worship. Before the dawn of history it had developed into a ritualistic cult, a complicated system of sacrifices, the performance of which was the class privilege of a guild of priests. In the hands of this priestly class the sacrificial cult became more and more elaborate, and occupied more and more the center of the stage. At first merely a means of gratification and propitiation of the gods, the sacrifice gradually became an end in itself, and finally, in the period succeeding the hymns of the Rig Veda, the gods became supernumeraries. The now all-important sacrifices no longer persuaded, but compelled them to do what the sacrificer desired; or else, at times, the sacrifice produced the desired result immediately, without any participation whatsoever on the part of the gods. The gods are even spoken of themselves as offering sacrifices; and it is said that they owe their divine position, or their very existence, to the sacrifice. This extreme glorification of the ritual performance appears in the period of the Brāhmaṇas, theological textbooks whose purpose is to expound the mystic meaning of the various rites. They are later in date than the Rig-Vedic hymns; and their religion, a pure magical ritualism, is the apotheosis, or the *reductio ad absurdum*, of the ritualistic nature-worship of the hymns.

Even in Rig-Vedic times the priestly ritual was so elaborate, and so expensive, that in the nature of things only rich men, mainly princes, could engage in it. It was therefore not only a hieratic but an aristocratic cult. The real religion of the great mass of the people was different. We find it portrayed best in the Atharva Veda. This is a collection of hymns, or rather magic charms, intended to accompany a mass of simpler rites and ceremonies which were not connected with the hieratic cult of the Rig Veda. Almost every conceivable human need and aspiration is represented by these popular performances. Their religious basis may be described as primitive animism, and their method of operation as simple magic. That is, they regard all creatures, things, powers, and even abstract principles, as volitional potencies or "spirits," or as animated by "spirits," which they seek to control by incantations and magic rites. They know also the higher gods of the Rig-Vedic pantheon, and likewise other gods which perhaps belonged at the start to aboriginal, non-"Aryan" tribes ("Aryan" is the name which the Vedic Hindus apply to themselves). But they invoke these gods after the manner of magic-mongers, much as medieval European incantations invoke the persons of the Trinity and Christian saints in connection with magic practices to heal a broken bone or to bring rain for the crops.

Later Hindu thought developed primarily out of the hieratic, Rig-Vedic religion; but it contains also quite a dash of lower, more popular beliefs. The separation of the two elements is by no means always easy. The truth seems to be that the speculations out of which the later forms of thought developed were carried on mainly by priests, adherents of the hieratic ritual religion. Almost all the intellectual leaders of the community belonged to the priestly class. But they were naturally — almost inevitably — influenced by the popular religion which surrounded them. Indeed, there was no opposition between the two types of religion, nor such a cleavage as our description may suggest. The followers of the hieratic cult also engaged in the practices that belonged to the more popular religion. This accounts for the constant infiltration from the "lower" sphere into the "higher," which we see going on at all periods. At times it is hard to decide whether a given new development is due to the intrusion of popular beliefs, or to internal evolution within the sphere of the priestly religion itself.

For we can clearly see the growth of certain new views within the Rig Veda itself. Out of the older ritualistic nature-worship, with its indefinite plurality of gods, arises in many Rig-Vedic hymns a new attitude, a sort of mitigated polytheism, to which has been given the name of *henotheism.* By this is meant a religious point of view which, when dealing for the moment with any particular god, seems to feel it as an insult to his dignity to admit the competition of other deities. And so, either the particular god of the moment is made to absorb all the others, who are declared to be manifestations of him; or else, he is given attributes which in strict logic could only be given to a sole monotheistic deity. Thus various Vedic gods are each at different times declared to be the creator, preserver, and animator of the universe, the sole ruler of all creatures, human and divine, and so on. Such hymns, considered separately, seem clearly to imply monotheism; but all that they really imply is a ritualistic henotheism. As each god comes upon the stage in the procession of rites, he is impartially granted this increasingly extravagant praise, until everything that could be said of all the gods collectively is said of each of them in turn, individually. We see that Vedic henotheism is rooted in the hieratic ritual, without which it perhaps would hardly have developed.

But it was not long before some advanced thinkers saw that such things as the creation of the world and the rulership over it could really be predicated only of one Personality. The question then arose, how to name and define that One? We might have expected that some one of the old gods would be erected into a truly monotheistic deity. But, perhaps because none of them seemed sufficiently superior to his fellows, perhaps for some other reason, this was not done. Instead, in a few late hymns of the Rig Veda we find various tentative efforts to establish a new deity in this supreme position. Different names are given to him: "the Lord of Creatures" (Prajāpati), "the All-maker" (Viśvakarman), and the like. As these names show, the new figure is rather abstract, and no longer ritualistic. Yet it is still personal. It is a *God* who creates, supports, and rules the world; a kind of Yahweh or Allah; not an impersonal First Cause. It is an attempt at monotheism, not yet monism.

These starts toward monotheism remained abortive, in the sense that they did not, at least directly, result in the establishment of a monotheistic religion comparable to that of the Hebrew people. Some centuries were to pass before such religions gained any strong foothold in India; and the connection between them and these early suggestions is remote and tenuous. The later religions owe their strength largely to other elements of more popular origin. Yet sporadic and more or less tentative suggestions of the sort continued to be made.

More striking, and more significant for the later development of Hindu philosophy, is a movement towards *monism* which appears, along with the monotheistic movement, even in the Rig Veda itself, tho only tentatively and very rarely. One or two Rig-Vedic hymns attempt to formulate the One in strictly impersonal, non-theistic terms. Among these I must mention the one hundred and twenty-ninth hymn of the tenth book of the Rig Veda, which to my mind is a very remarkable production, considering its time and place. This "hymn" (for so we can hardly help calling it, since it is found in the "hymn-book" of the Rig Veda) also seeks to explain the universe as evolving out of One; but its One is no longer a god. It knows no Yahweh or Allah, any more than the ritualistic Indra or Varuṇa. It definitely brushes aside all gods, not indeed denying their existence, but declaring that they are all of late and secondary origin; they know nothing of the beginnings of things. The First Principle of this hymn is "That One" (*tad ekam*). It is of neuter gender, as it were lest some theologian should get hold of it and insist on falling down and worshiping it. It is not only impersonal and non-theistic, but absolutely uncharacterizable and indescribable, without qualities or attributes, even negative ones. It was "neither existent nor non-existent." To seek to know it is hopeless; in the last two verses of the hymn (there are only seven in all) the author relapses into a negative style of expression which remains characteristic of Hindu higher thought in certain moods. While the later Upaniṣads often try to describe the One all-inclusively, by saying that it is *everything*, that it contains all possible and conceivable characteristics; still in some of their deepest moments they too prefer the negative statement *neti, neti*[1] — "No, no." To apply to it any description is to limit and bound that which is limitless and boundless. It cannot be described; it cannot be known.

But the ancient Hindu thinkers could never resign themselves to this negation. Even if they sometimes recognized that they could not, in the nature of things, know the Unknowable, still their restless speculation kept returning to the struggle again and again, from ever varied points of attack. In the Rig Veda itself, in one of its latest hymns (10.90), appears the first trace of a strain of monistic thought which is of the greatest importance for later Hindu philosophy: the universe is treated as parallel in nature to the human personality. The First Principle in this hymn is called Puruṣa, that is, "Man" or "Person." From the several parts of this cosmic Person are derived, by a still rather crude process of evolution, all existing things. The significance of this lies in its anticipation of the Upaniṣadic view of the identity of the human soul (later called *ātman*, literally "self," as a rule) with the universal principle.

Other, later Vedic texts, especially the Atharva Veda, also contain speculative materials. They are extremely varied in character; they testify to the restlessness and tentativeness which we have seen as a characteristic of all early Hindu thought. At times they seem monotheistic in tendency. The "Lord of Creatures," Prajāpati, of the Rig Veda, appears again and again, as a kind of demiurge; and other names are invented for the same or a similar figure, such as the "Establisher," Dhātar, or the "Arranger," Vidhātar, or "He that is in the Highest," Parameṣṭhin. But never does such a figure attain anything like the definite dignity which we associate with a genuine monotheistic deity. And more often the interest centers around less personal, more abstract entities, either physical or metaphysical, or more or less both at once. The sun, especially under the mystic name of Rohita, "the Ruddy One," enjoys a momentary glory in several Atharva-Vedic charms, which invest him with the functions of a cosmic principle. Or the world is developed out of water; we are reminded of Thales, the first of the Greek philosophers. The wind, regarded as the most subtle of physical elements and as the "life-breath" (*prāṇa*) of the universe, plays at times a like role, and by being compared with man's life-breath it contributes to the development of the cosmic "Person" (Puruṣa) of the Rig Veda into the later Ātman or Soul (of man) as the Supreme One. The word *ātman*

[1] Bṛhad Āraṇyaka Upaniṣad 3.9.26, and in other places.

itself seems actually to be used in this way in one or two late verses of the Atharva Veda.[2] The power of Time (*kāla*), or of Desire (*kāma*) — a sort of cosmic Will, reminding us of Schopenhauer — is elsewhere treated as the force behind the evolution of the universe. Or, still more abstractly, the world-all is derived from a hardly defined "Support," that is, a "Fundamental Principle" (*skambha*), on which everything rests. These and other shadowy figures flit across the stage of later Vedic speculation. Individually, few of them have enough definiteness or importance to merit much attention. But in the mass they are of the greatest value for one who would follow the development of Hindu speculation as a whole.

The real underlying motive and rationale of all this "monism," this seeking for a single principle in the universe, cannot be understood without reference to the principle of *identification* as it appears in early Vedic texts; most clearly in the Brāhmaṇas (above, p. 111). A very striking feature of these works is their passion for identification of one thing with another, on the slenderest possible basis; indeed, often on no basis at all that we can discover. The purpose was strictly practical; more specifically, magical. It was to get results by setting cosmic forces in motion. To this end a cosmic force was said to "be" this or that other thing, which other thing we can control. "By grasping or controlling one of the two identified entities, the possessor of the mystic knowledge as to their identity has power over the other, which is in fact no other"[3] but really the same. For instance, "the cow is breath"; I control a cow, therefore I control breath, my own life-breath, or some one else's. That is the only reason for the fantastic identification. We want to control, let us say, the breath of life, in ourselves or some one else (perhaps an enemy): so we earnestly and insistently identify it with something that we *can* control, and the trick is turned. It required only a slight extension of this to arrive at the notion that if we can only "know" the one principle of the whole universe, the one which is to be *identified* with "all," with every thing that is, we shall then control all, and be able to deal with the universe as we please.[4] So all Vedic speculation is eminently practical. As we said above, metaphysical truth *per se* and for its own sake is not its object. Earnest and often profound tho these thinkers are, they never lose sight for long of their practical aim, which is to control, by virtue of their superior knowledge, the cosmic forces which they study. That is why so many of their speculations are imbedded in the Atharva Veda, a book of magic spells, which to our minds would seem the most inappropriate place possible.

[2] 10.8.43, 44.

[3] H. Oldenberg, *Vorwissenschaftliche Wissenschaft*, Göttingen, 1919, p. 110.

[4] See my article, "The Upaniṣads, what do they seek and why?" *Journal of the American Oriental Society*, 49.97 ff.

It might seem to follow from this that the speculative activity of this period belonged to the popular sphere represented by the religion of the Atharva Veda, more than to the ritualistic cult that was the heir of the Rig Veda. But I think there is evidence to the contrary, However appropriate to the spirit of the popular religion it seemed in some respects, this activity was carried on mainly by the priests of the hieratic ritual. And this fact, which for various reasons seems to me indubitable, finds a striking concrete expression in a philosophic term developed in this period which deserves special consideration.

Among all the varied formulations of the First and Supreme Principle, none recurs more constantly thruout the later Vedic texts than the *brahman*. The oldest meaning of this word seems to be "holy knowledge," "sacred utterance," or (what to primitive man is the same thing) its concrete expression, "hymn" or "incantation." It is applied both to the ritual hymns of the Rig Veda and to the magic charms of the Atharva Veda. Any holy, mystic utterance is *brahman*. This is the regular, if not the exclusive, meaning which the word has in the Rig Veda. But from the point of view of those times, this definition implies far more than it would suggest to our minds. The spoken word had a mysterious, supernatural power; it contained within itself the essence of the thing denoted. To "know the *name*" of anything was to control the thing. The *word* means wisdom, knowledge; and knowledge, as we have seen, was (magic) power. So *brahman*, the "holy word," soon came to mean the mystic power inherent in the holy word.

But to the later Vedic ritualists, this holy word was the direct expression and embodiment of the ritual religion, and as such a cosmic power of the first magnitude. The ritual religion, and hence its verbal expression, the *brahman*, was omnipotent; it was "all." All human desires and aspirations were accessible to him who mastered it. All other cosmic forces, even the greatest of natural and supernatural powers, were dependent upon it. The gods themselves, originally the beneficiaries of the cult, became its helpless mechanical agents, or were left out of account altogether as useless middlemen. The cult was the direct controlling force of the universe. And the *brahman* was the spirit, the expression, of the cult; nay, it *was* the cult, mystically speaking, because the word and the thing were one; he who knew the word, knew and controlled the thing. Therefore, he who knew the *brahman* knew and controlled the whole universe. It is no wonder, then, that in the later Vedic texts (not yet in the Rig Veda) we find the *brahman* frequently mentioned as the primal principle [5] and as the ruling and guiding spirit of the universe. It is a thoroly ritualistic notion, inconceivable ex-

[5] "There is nothing more ancient or higher than this *brahman*," Śatapatha Brāhmaṇa, 10.3.5.11.

cept as an outgrowth of the theories of the ritualistic cult, but very simple and as it were self-evident from the point of view of the ritualists. The overwhelming prominence and importance of the *brahman* in later Vedic speculation seems, therefore, a striking proof of the fact that this speculation was at least in large part a product of ritualistic, priestly circles.

Not content with attempts to identify the One, the Vedic thinkers also try to define His, or Its, relation to the empiric world. Here again their suggestions are many and varied. Often the One is a sort of demiurge, a Creator, Father, First Cause. Such theistic expressions may be used of impersonal monistic names for the One as well as of more personal, quasi-monotheistic ones. The One is compared to a carpenter or a smith; he joins or smelts the world into being. Or his act is like an act of generation; he begets all beings. Still more interestingly, his creative activity is compared to a sacrifice, a ritual performance, or to prayer, or religious fervor (*dhī*, *tapas*). This obviously ritualistic imagery appears even in the Rig Veda itself, in several of its philosophic hymns. In the Puruṣa hymn, already referred to, the universe is derived from the sacrifice of the cosmic Person, the Puruṣa; the figure is of the dismemberment of a sacrificial animal; from each of the members of the cosmic Puruṣa evolved a part of the existing world. The performers of this cosmogonic sacrifice are "the gods," — inconsistently, of course, for the gods have already been declared to be secondary to the Puruṣa, who transcends all existing things. In later Vedic times we repeatedly meet with such ritualistic expressions. They confirm our feeling that we are dealing with priests.

We see from what has just been said of the Puruṣa hymn that the One — here the Puruṣa, the cosmic "Person" or "man" — may be regarded as the material source (*causa materialis*) as well as the creator (*causa efficiens*) of the world. All evolves out of it, or is a part of it; but frequently, as in the Puruṣa hymn, it is *more* than all empiric existence; it transcends all things, which form, or derive from, but a part of it. Again, it is often spoken of as the ruler, controller, or lord of all. Or, it is the foundation, fundament, upon which all is based, which supports all. Still more significant are passages which speak of the One as subtly pervading all, as air or ether or space (*ākāśa*) pervades the physical universe, and animating all, as the breath of life (*prāṇa*) is regarded as both pervading and animating the human body.

Such expressions as this last lead to a modification, with mitigation of the crudity, of the above-noted parallelism between man, the microcosm, and the universe, the macrocosm, which as we have seen dates from late Rig-Vedic times. In the Puruṣa hymn of the Rig Veda we find a crude evolution of various parts of the physical universe from the parts of the physical body of the cosmic "Man." But in the later Vedic texts the feeling grows that man's nature is not accounted for by dissecting his physical body —

and, correspondingly, that there must be something more in the universe than the sum total of its physical elements. What is that "something more" in man? Is it the "life-breath" or "life-breaths" (*prāṇa*), which seem to be in and thru various parts of the human body and to be the principle of man's life (since they leave the body at death)? So many Vedic thinkers believed. What, then, is the corresponding "life-breath" of the universe? Obviously the wind, say some. Others think of it as the *ākāśa*, "ether," or "space." But even these presently seem too physical, too material. On the human side, too, it begins to be evident that the "life-breath," like its cosmic counterpart the wind, is in reality physical. Surely the essential Man must be something else. What then? Flittingly, here and there, it is suggested that it may be man's "desire" or "will" (*kāma*), or his "mind" (*manas*), or something else of a more or less "psychological" nature. But already in the Atharva Veda, and with increasing frequency later, we find as an expression for the real, essential part of Man the word *ātman* used. *Ātman* means simply "self"; it is used familiarly as a reflexive pronoun, like the German *sich*. One could hardly get a more abstract term for that which is left when everything unessential is deducted from man, and which is at the same time to be considered the principle of his life, the living soul that pervades his being. And, carrying on the parallelism, we presently find mention of the *ātman*, self or soul, of the universe. The texts do not content themselves with that; they continue to speculate as to what that "soul" of the universe is. But these speculations tend to become more and more remote from purely physical elements. Increasing partiality is shown for such metaphysical expressions as "the existent," or "that which is" (*sat*),[6] or again "the non-existent" (*asat*); in the Rig-Vedic hymn 10.129 we were told that in the beginning there was "neither existent nor non-existent," but later we find both "the existent" and "the non-existent" used as expressions for the first principle. But perhaps the favorite formula in later Vedic times for the soul of the universe is the originally ritualistic one of the *brahman*.

If we remember the Brāhmaṇa principle of identification by mystic knowledge for purposes of magical control, set forth above, we shall now be able to understand the standard answer given in the Upaniṣads to the question "With what shall we identify the one thing, by knowing which all is known?" That answer is: "With the soul, the *ātman*, of man." Obviously; for whether it be called *Brahman*, or the existent, or what-not, the

[6] Compare the Greek τὸ ὄν or τὸ ὄντως ὄν, "that which (really) is," and, for a less exact parallel, the Kantian *Ding an sich*. But the "existent," the "being," that which (really) is, whether in man or in the universe, was probably not so abstract or metaphysical as we feel the corresponding western phrases. The Sanskrit word must be understood from the magical standpoint which I have described.

One is naturally the essential self or "soul," *ātman*, of the universe. If it is *ātman*, and my soul, my real self, is also *ātman*, then is not the mystic identification ready-made? By "knowing" the one I may "know" — *and control* — the other. And surely there is nothing which I control more obviously and perfectly than my own "self." If now I "know" that the Brahman, which is the *ātman* of the universe, is my own *ātman*, then not only do I control the fundamental principle of the universe, because knowledge is magic power; but even more than that, I *am* the fundamental principle of the universe, by mystic identification. For this double reason, there is nothing beyond my grasp. Thus the knowledge of the One which is All, and its identification with the human soul, is a short-cut to the satisfaction of all desires, the freedom from all fear and danger and sorrow.

CHAPTER III

The Upanisads, and the Fundamental Doctrines of Later Hindu Thought

The Upaniṣads are the earliest Hindu treatises, other than single hymns or brief passages, which deal with philosophic subjects. They are formally parts of the Veda,[1] — the last offshoots of Vedic literature. The dry bones of the Vedic ritual cult rattle about in them in quite a noisy fashion at times, and seriously strain our patience and our charity. But they also contain the apotheosis, the New Testament, of Vedic philosophy. In them the struggling speculations which we have briefly sketched in the last chapter reach their highest development. They do not, be it noted, receive any final, systematic codification. That came much later. They are still tentative, fluid, and, one may fairly say, unstable; they are frequently inconsistent with each other and with themselves. They contain no system, but starts toward various different systems. Later Hindu thought utilized these starts and developed them into the various systematic philosophies of later times — Sāṃkhya, Vedānta, and the rest. In fact, there are few important terms of later Hindu philosophical or religious thought which are not at least foreshadowed in the Upaniṣads. They are the connecting link between the Veda and later Hinduism; the last word of the one, the prime source of the other.

In this chapter, I wish to deal with the Upaniṣads mostly from the latter point of view: to show how they reveal the early stages of the fundamental postulates of later Hindu thought. While the views reproduced in this chapter are all found in the early Upaniṣads (except where the contrary is stated), we also find in them expressions of quite different views, which approach much more closely the older Vedic speculations. The relation of the Upaniṣads to those earlier speculations may, in general, be described by saying that while the Upaniṣads carry their inquiries along essentially the same lines, and are actuated by the same basic belief in the mystic, magic power of knowledge, their interests become increasingly anthropocentric and less cosmo-physical or ritualistic. Explanations of the cosmic absolute in purely physical terms, and speculations about the esoteric meaning of ritual entities, while they still occur, become less prominent; speculations on the nature and fate of man, and explanations of the universe in human or quasi-human terms, increase in frequency. Thus one of the most striking

[1] At least the older and more genuine ones are that; we may ignore for our present purpose the numerous late and secondary works which call themselves Upaniṣads.

dogmas in the Upaniṣads is that the human soul or self *is* the Absolute ("that art thou";[2] "I am Brahman";[3] "it [the universal Brahman] is thy self, that is within everything";[4] "that which rests in all things and is distinct from all things, which all things know not, of which all things are the body [that is, the material representation or form], which controls all things within, that is thy self [*ātman*], the immortal Inner Controller").[5] All that is outside of this Self is at times viewed as created by, or emitted from, It (as in dreams the Self seems to create a dream-world and to live in it).[6] At other times the sharp line drawn between the Self and material nature, that is all that is not Self, is made to preclude any genetic relation between the two.[7]

The reason for the identification of the human soul with the principle of the universe was suggested in the last chapter, but I shall summarize it once more in words which I have used elsewhere.[8] "The Upaniṣads seek to know the real truth about the universe, not for its own sake; not for the mere joy of knowledge; not as an abstract speculation; but simply because they conceive such knowledge as a short-cut to the control of every cosmic power. The possessor of such knowledge will be in a position to satisfy his any desire. He will be free from old age and death, from danger and sorrow, from all the ills that flesh is heir to. By knowledge of the One that is All, and by mystically identifying his own self with that One which is All, he has, like that One, the All in his control. Knowledge, true esoteric knowledge, is the magic key to omnipotence, absolute power. By it one becomes autonomous. Vedic philosophy . . . is simply an attempt to gain at one stroke all possible human ends, by *knowing*, once for all, the essential truth of the entire cosmos. If all can be known at once, and especially if it can be mystically identified with one's own 'soul,' then all will be controlled, and there will be no need of half-way measures; no need of attempting by magic

[2] Chāndogya Upaniṣad 6.8.7, etc.

[3] Bṛhad Āraṇyaka Upaniṣad 1.4.10, etc.

[4] *Ibid.*, 3.4.1.

[5] *Ibid.*, 3.7.15.

[6] *Ibid.*, 4.3.10. According to several Upaniṣad passages the soul performs this creative act by a sort of mystic, quasi-magic power, sometimes called *māyā*, that is, "artifice"; it is a word sometimes applied to sorcery, and to tricks and stratagems of various kinds. The Bhagavad Gītā similarly speaks of the Deity as appearing in material nature by His *māyā*, His mystic power. This does not mean (in my opinion; some scholars take the contrary view) that the world outside of the self is illusory, without real existence, as the later Vedānta philosophy maintains; *māyā*, I think, is not used in the Vedāntic sense of "world-illusion" until many centuries later.

[7] Thus foreshadowing the later dualistic systems, such as classical Sāṃkhya and Yoga, which recognize matter and soul as two eternal and eternally independent principles — a doctrine which is familiarly accepted in the Bhagavad Gītā.

[8] *Journal of the American Oriental Society*, 49.118.

to gain this or that special desideratum [which minor and special desiderata are nevertheless constantly sought in the Upaniṣads, by a natural inconsistency which only helps to prove my point]. . . . The Brahman, as an expression for the supreme power of the universe, is simply this same mystic knowledge. . . ."

In view of this, it is not strange that the attention of the Upaniṣadic thinkers is more and more centered upon the human soul. Other things are important as they are related to it. And — while its origin and past history remain objects of interest — we find an increasing amount of attention paid to its future fate. The practical purpose of speculation reasserts itself emphatically in the question, how can man control his own destiny? What is man's *summum bonum*, and how shall he attain it? It is out of such questions and the answers to them that the basic postulates of later Hindu thought develop.

In early Vedic times the objects of human desire are the ordinary ones which natural man seeks the world over: wealth, pleasures, power over his fellows, long life, and offspring; and finally, since death puts an end to the enjoyment of all these, immortality. Immortality, however, can only be hoped for in a future existence, since all life on this earth is seen to end in death. So the Vedic poets hope for some sort of heavenly and eternal life after death. But presently they begin to be uneasy lest perchance death might interfere with that future life, also. The fear of this "re-death" becomes, in what we may call the Middle Vedic period (the Brāhmaṇas), a very prominent feature. Combined with this is the growing belief in the imperishability of the *ātman*, the Self or Soul, the essential part of the living being. These two views are not mutually contradictory. Death remains, as a very disagreeable experience — no less disagreeable if it must be undergone more than once — even tho it does not destroy the Soul but only brings it over into a new existence. What pleasure can man take in wealth, power, and offspring, if this sword of Damocles is constantly hanging over him, threatening to deprive him of all, and to launch him upon some new and untried existence? Moreover, that future existence may be no better than the present one. Possibly under the influence of popular animism, which sees "souls" similar to the human soul in all parts of nature, the future life is brought down from heaven to this earth. And so, in the early Upaniṣads, we find quite definite statements of the theory of rebirth or transmigration, which was to remain thru all future time an axiom to practically all Hindus. According to this, the Soul is subject to an indefinite series of existences, in various material forms or "bodies," either in this world or in various imaginary worlds. The Bhagavad Gītā expresses this universal Hindu belief in the form of two similes. It says that one existence follows another just as different stages of life — childhood, young manhood, and old age — follow one another in this life.[9] Or again, just as one lays off old garments and dons new ones, so the Soul lays off an old, worn-out body and puts on a new one.[10] One of the oldest Upaniṣads uses the simile of a grass-leech, which crawls to the end of a blade of grass and then "gathers itself together" to pass over to another blade of grass; so the Soul at death "gathers itself together" and passes over to a new existence.[11]

The Upaniṣads also begin to combine with this doctrine of an indefinite series of reincarnations the old belief in retribution for good and evil deeds in a life after death; a belief which prevailed among the people of Vedic India, as all over the world. With the transfer of the future life from a mythical other world to this earth, and with the extension or multiplication of it to an indefinite series of future lives more or less like the present life, the way was prepared for the characteristically Hindu doctrine of "karma" (*karman*) or "deed." This doctrine, which is also axiomatic to the Hindus, teaches that the state of each existence of each individual is absolutely conditioned and determined by that individual's morality in previous existences. A man is exactly what he has made himself and what he therefore deserves to be. An early Upaniṣad says: "Just as (the Soul) is (in this life) of this or that sort; just as it acts, just as it operates, even so precisely it becomes (in the next life). If it acts well it becomes good; if it acts ill it becomes evil. As a result of right action it becomes what is good; as a result of evil action it becomes what is evil." [12] In short, the law of the conservation of energy is rigidly applied to the moral world. Every action, whether good or bad, must have its result for the doer. If in the present life a man is on the whole good, his next existence is better by just so much as his good deeds have outweighed his evil deeds. He becomes a great and noble man, or a king, or perhaps a god (the gods, like men, are subject to the law of transmigration). Conversely, a wicked man is reborn as a person of low position, or as an animal, or, in cases of exceptional depravity, he may fall to existence in hell. And all this is not carried out by decree of some omnipotent and sternly just Power. It is a natural law. It operates of itself just as much as the law of gravitation. It is therefore wholly dispassionate, neither merciful nor vindictive. It is absolutely inescapable; but at the same time it never cuts off hope. A man is what he has made himself; but by that same token he may make himself what he will. The soul tormented in the lowest hell may raise himself in time to the highest heaven, simply by doing right. Perfect justice is made the basic law of the universe. It is a principle of great moral grandeur and perfection.

[9] ii. 13.

[10] ii. 22.

[11] Bṛhad Āraṇyaka Upaniṣad, 4.4.3.

[12] *Ibid.*, 4.4.5.

The Upaniṣads go farther than this in anticipating later Hindu views of the Soul's progress. One of the earliest of them contains this passage: "This Spirit of Man consists simply of *desire*. As is his desire, so is his resolve; as is his resolve, so is the deed (*karman*) that he does; as is the deed that he does, so is that (fate) which he attains unto."[13] The root of action, and so the determining cause of man's future fate, is his "desire." It follows that if man's desires can be properly regulated, he can be led to his true goal. This remains a fundamental tenet of later Hinduism.

It might seem that the glorification of the Soul as the center of the universe should be a comforting and inspiring thought. And, indeed, the Upaniṣads and later Hindu works describe the perfections of the Soul in inspiring and even ecstatic terms. But the practical effect of all this upon the Hindu attitude towards our present life was just the opposite. It only served to emphasize the contrast between the Soul and all that is not Soul, that is, all material or empiric existence. "Whatever is other than That (the Soul) is evil," says an early Upaniṣad.[14] Soon this crystallizes into a definitely and thoroly pessimistic view of life. All existence, in the ordinary empiric sense, is inherently worthless and base and evil. Pleasures are both transitory and illusory. Death is not only an evil in itself, which threatens us at every moment, but also it leads only to further existence, that is, to further misery. True joy and peace can only be found in the Self.

Accordingly, the perfected man is he "*whose desire is the Soul*, whose desire is satisfied, who has no desire" (other than the Soul; that is, who is free from ordinary, worldly desires),[15] who "is beyond desire, has dispensed with evil, knows no fear, is free from sorrow."[16] As long as a man is affected by desire (other than the desire for the Soul's perfection, which, as just indicated, is the same as having *no* desire), this leads him to "resolve" and to "action," which must have its fruit in continued material existence; and all material existence is evil.

The estate of this perfected man is most commonly described as attainment of, going to, or union with the One — which may be called Brahman, or the Ātman (the Self or Soul), or some synonym. It is not non-existence, according to the Upaniṣads; for the soul is immortal, and cannot cease to be. It is sometimes even declared to be a conscious state; but this is immediately qualified by saying that tho the soul still has the faculties of seeing, knowing, and so on, there is no object for these faculties to act upon, so that after all

[13] *Ibid.*, 4.4.5.

[14] *Ibid.*, 3.4.2.

[15] These include, typically, sensual desires of all kinds, and desire for continued existence in rebirths.

[16] Bṛhad Āraṇyaka Upaniṣad, 4.4.6; 4.3.22.

it is to all intents and purposes a state of unconsciousness.[17] As the soul is one with the universal subject, than which there is then no other, there can be no object, and hence no activity of the senses or mental faculties. So at other times the texts plainly say "there is no consciousness after death (for the perfected soul)."[18] They treat it as similar to the state of deep and dreamless sleep, which is indeed at times said to be a temporary union with the One, and so a foretaste of that perfected condition.[19] It is natural that such a state should be associated with bliss; for while the waking man has no recollection of consciousness or anything else as having existed in sound sleep, still he awakes from it feeling refreshed and perhaps with a vague impression of having been in some sort of remote and happy state. At any rate, the Upaniṣads leave no doubt that there is in this union with the One a total cessation of desires, of evil, of sorrow — in short, of ordinary, empiric, worldly existence, which is characterized by desires, evil, and sorrow. But not content with that, they describe it as a state of pure and ecstatic bliss, infinitely surpassing all human joys, indeed far exceeding the power of man to conceive it.[20]

Later Hindu religions and philosophies call this state by the well-known name *nirvāṇa*. This means "extinction," originally of a fire or flame; then of the flames of desire, as the cause of continued rebirth. Some later sects, such as the Buddhists, have been represented as meaning by it also literal extinction of life, of existence in any form; but with more than doubtful propriety. At any rate, even in Buddhist texts *nirvāṇa* is described as a state of blissful ecstasy. It makes no difference if, with the later Sāṃkhya, one denies the world-soul and merely regards the perfected individual souls as existing separately, independent of each other and of matter; still the same descriptions are used. All the later variations in metaphysical theory (some of them adumbrated in the Upaniṣads) make no difference in the view of the perfected state as a kind of pure and — so to speak — unconscious consciousness, and transcendent bliss. The Bhagavad Gītā uses the word *nirvāṇa* several times, generally in the compound *brahmanirvāṇa*, "extinction in Brahman," or "the extinction which is Brahman." More commonly it uses vaguer terms to describe the goal which means salvation — such expressions as "perfection," "the highest goal," "the supreme state" or "My (God's) estate." Or it simply says "he attains Me (God)," or "he attains Brahman"; that is, the perfected man becomes united with God or with Brahman. Details as to the nature of that state are wholly wanting in the Gītā, if we except such vague expressions as "that highest station of Mine, to which having gone one does not return, is not illumined by sun or moon or fire"[21] — implying that it shines by its own light. We are not told how

[17] *Ibid.*, 4.5.15; 4.3.23 ff.
[18] *Ibid.*, 4.5.13.
[19] *Ibid.*, 4.3.19 ff.
[20] *Ibid.*, 4.3.32, 33.
[21] 15.6.

the Gītā regarded the state of a man who had gained this position. All that seems clear is that it was regarded as some sort of real existence, not as total and absolute annihilation.

The way to attain this state of perfection, as to attain anything else, is, according to the usual Upaniṣad doctrine, by true knowledge. Knowledge is the magic talisman that opens all doors. He who knows anything, controls it; and so, he who knows the supreme truth thereby becomes master of it, and gains the highest state. "He who knows that supreme Brahman, unto Brahman he goes."[22] Similar expressions appear constantly thruout the whole Upaniṣad literature. This comes as near as anything to being a universal doctrine of the Upaniṣads. It is furthermore a doctrine which is of fundamental importance in all later Hindu thought. All the later systems make it their prime business to point the way to human salvation; and one may say in general that their methods are primarily and originally intellectual, or, perhaps better, intuitive. They teach that man shall be saved thru the realization of the supreme truth. In their formulations of that truth they differ, of course, among themselves; that is the reason for the plurality of systems. But they usually state, or at least imply, the omnipotence of knowledge; and conversely they usually emphasize the fact that ignorance (*avidyā*) is the root of evil. Characteristic of them all is the Buddhist formula, which says that ignorance is the cause of desire; desire leads to action; and action must have its fruit, as we have seen, in continued existence, all of which is evil.

Even *good* deeds are still deeds, and must have their fruit, according to the doctrine of "karma." And to attain the *summum bonum* man must get rid of all deeds, of all karma. Therefore, while most if not all Hindu systems teach a practical morality, they also teach that no degree of morality, however perfect, can lead to final salvation. In this, too, they are anticipated by the Upaniṣads. The perfect soul is "beyond good and evil."[23] Neither good nor evil can affect him. At times the Upaniṣads seem even to say or imply that when a man has attained enlightenment, he can do what he likes without fear of results. This somewhat dangerous doctrine is, however, not typical, and is probably to be regarded only as a strained and exaggerated manner of saying that the truly enlightened soul cannot, in the very nature of things, do an evil deed. If he could, he would not be truly enlightened; for "he who has not ceased from evil conduct cannot attain Him (the Ātman) by intelligence."[24] This is similar to the Socratic notion that the truly wise man must inevitably be virtuous. The difference is that the Upaniṣads regard even virtue, as well as vice, as transcended by perfect

[22] Muṇḍaka Upaniṣad, 3.2.9; Kauṣītaki Upaniṣad, 1. 4.
[23] Kauṣītaki Upaniṣad, 1.4; compare Bṛhad Āraṇyaka Upaniṣad, 4.3.22, etc.
[24] Kaṭha Upaniṣad, 2.24.

knowledge; the possessor thereof passes beyond both, and rises to a plane on which moral terms simply have no meaning. Morality applies only in the world of karma, the world of ordinary empiric existence, which the enlightened man has left behind him. In the final state of the perfected man, as we have seen, there can be, strictly speaking, no action; so how can there be either moral or immoral action? The attitude of the Upaniṣads, and following them of most later Hindu systems, is then that morality has only a negative importance, and in the last analysis none whatever, in man's struggle for salvation. Immorality is a sign of imperfection; it can only be due to the prevalence in the soul of ignorance, causing desire, leading to action and rebirth. It must be got rid of. But it will fall away of itself with the attainment of true wisdom. And no amount of good deeds will bring that wisdom which alone can lead to release. Good deeds result in less unhappy existences, but that is all; salvation is release from all empiric existence. This does not prevent the teaching of a system of practical ethics, for the guidance of those who have not yet attained enlightenment. In actual practice, most Hindu sects inculcate very lofty moral principles; and many of them devote much attention thereto. But theoretically, at least, such things do not concern their fundamental aims.

Yet at times morality is spoken of as if it had a positive, if only qualified, value in preparing the soul for the reception of enlightenment. The fact is that the strictly intellectual or intuitional position is hard for the ordinary man to master. He needs the encouragement of more concrete aims, or helps toward the final aim. Many of the later sects recognize this, either implicitly or explicitly, and so do not hold strictly to the position that "knowledge," that is, immediate perception of the metaphysical truth, is the sole and exclusive means of salvation. Even the Upanisads do not quite do this, tho they come closer to it than many later systems. Despite the popular and even primitive background of their intellectualism, its relation to the old idea of the magic power of knowledge, the speculation of the Upaniṣads in its highest forms reached a point which must have placed it out of touch with the beliefs of most of the people. "Knowledge" of the abstract truth about the Soul proves a very different matter from "knowledge" of the things which are the ordinary aims of magic, when the human being tries to grasp it. Any man can "know" the "name" of his enemy, or of the disease which afflicts him, and by that "knowledge" can seek to cast a spell over them. But only a rare thinker can "know" the absolute metaphysical Truth, so that it is an ever-present illumination of his whole being,[25]

[25] "By a rare chance may a man see him (the Soul); by a rare chance likewise may another declare him; and by a rare chance may another hear (of) him. But even when he has heard (of) him, no one whatsoever knows him." Bhagavad Gītā, ii. 29; quoted from Kaṭha Upaniṣad, 2.7.

and this is what he must do in order to have the true "knowledge" that brings control of his own soul, of his destiny — the "knowledge" that means salvation. For ordinary human nature, there is needed a process of education, of discipline, which shall lead up to this enlightenment. Various sects make use of morality in this way, as a preliminary help. It purifies the soul and prepares it for enlightenment. Many Upaniṣad passages imply such a position, at least by saying that the wicked cannot hope for true knowledge — even tho other passages speak of knowledge as a sort of magic power by which one "sloughs off sin, as a snake sloughs off its skin." [26]

There are other preliminary steps or practices which various sects regard as useful in preparing the soul for the reception of the enlightenment which will finally bring release. And in some of the later Hindu sects these preliminary steps become so prominent that they obscure, or almost obliterate, what was originally the true goal — the attainment of metaphysical knowledge. Of these avenues of approach to knowledge, which however occasionally lead off into seductive bypaths, the chief, in addition to righteous conduct, are two. One is devotion to the personality of some god or prophet, who is regarded as a kind of personal savior or helper on the way to salvation. The other is the practice of asceticism in some form or other, regarded as an approach to a state of inaction (and so to the ideal, since all actions lead to rebirth), and also as helping to prepare for enlightenment by freeing the individual from attachment to the world, by gradually conquering the natural desires of the flesh.

The first of these two secondary methods, as we may call them, plays a very small rôle in the older Upaniṣads. The Upaniṣads recognize no prophet who could occupy the place which the Buddha holds for his followers as a personal Savior, quite analogous to the places of Jesus and Mohammed in Christianity and Islam. And most of them, particularly the earliest, do not speak of the One — Brahman, or Ātman, or the Existent, or whatever they call It — in sufficiently personal terms to make it easy to treat It as exercising grace in saving men, or as the object of any very personal devotion on the part of men. But for the Bhagavad Gītā, which is frankly monotheistic,[27] the case is very different; and we shall find that in it the "grace of God" is repeatedly spoken of as singling out His elect and bringing them to salvation by His divine choice. And no means for attaining salvation is more emphasized in the Gītā than *bhakti*, "devotion" to God, or fervent love of Him. Originally, no doubt, this devotion was to lead to knowledge, intellectual enlightenment, and so to release. But the intermediate step is often

[26] Praśna Upaniṣad, 5.5.

[27] This is certainly a reasonable statement in dealing with a work in which the principal speaker is represented as an incarnation of the Supreme Deity; altho there are not wanting in the Gītā, as we shall see in Chapter VI, passages in which the First Principle seems to be spoken of in impersonal, monistic terms.

lost sight of in the Gītā and in similar later works; they not infrequently speak of ecstatic love of God as leading immediately to absorption in Him, which is their conception of salvation. It is interesting to note, then, that even this position, contrary tho it is to the usual spirit of the Upaniṣads, finds expression in them, and precisely in two of them which were pretty certainly known to the author of the Gītā. One speaks of enlightenment as coming "by the grace of God," and recommends "devotion" (*bhakti*) to Him as a means for attaining it.[28] The other speaks of "beholding the greatness of the Soul (*ātman*) by the grace of the Creator (*dhātar*)," [29] and shortly after this the same text, not even using the term "Creator" or "God," or any other personal expression for the Supreme, says that "this Soul (*ātman*; here the Universal Soul) is not to be attained by instruction, by intellect, or by much holy learning; He is to be attained only by him whom He chooses; for him He reveals His own form." [30]

The other "secondary method" of gaining enlightenment, the method of withdrawal from the world by some form of asceticism, is more complicated in its history. In the oldest periods of Vedic speculation we hear much of what is called *tapas*. Already in the great monistic hymn of the Rig Veda, 10.129, the One is produced out of the primal chaos by the power of *tapas*. The word means literally "heat," and in cosmogonic connections it undoubtedly suggests the creative warmth that is symbolized by the brooding of a bird over its eggs. Belief in the development of the universe out of a cosmic egg appears not infrequently in early Hindu cosmogonies, and with it is clearly associated belief in *tapas*, warmth, as a force of cosmic evolution. But in religious language the same word had the figurative meaning of "religious, devotional fervor." It is the inspiration of the priest or holy man. It was thus nearly related to the notion of *brahman*, the holy word as the quintessence of religious spirit. It is possible that it had a partly physical connotation in this sense, too; the religious fervor probably was sometimes brought on or increased by physical exertion; and even the sacrificial ritual itself, being performed over the sacred fire, resulted in literal, physical "heat" for the officiating priests (the texts refer to this specifically). For these various reasons the power of *tapas*, "warmth" or "fervor," is prominently mentioned in early Vedic cosmogonies as a cosmic force. Sometimes it is made a sort of First Principle itself. More often the Creator is spoken of as "exercising *tapas*" in creating the universe.

But about the time of the early Upaniṣads the word *tapas* began to acquire a new connotation. From this period seems to date the development in

[28] Śvetāśvatara Upaniṣad, 6.21, 23. This is a comparatively late Upaniṣad, probably not much older than the Gītā; there are various good reasons for believing that it was known to the Gītā's author.

[29] Kaṭha Upaniṣad, 2.20. The Gītā has several verbal quotations from this Upaniṣad.

[30] *Ibid.*, 2.23.

India of a recognized class of hermits or monks, men who renounced the world and lived a life devoted to meditation or some form of asceticism. The prominence of such people in later India is well known. They do not appear clearly in the early Vedic texts; and their appearance in large numbers is certainly related to the growth of world-weariness among the Hindu intellectuals, which accompanied and signalized the general views of life outlined in this chapter. If all ordinary life is vanity and vexation of spirit, and the only hope of salvation lies in knowledge of the Soul, which is to be attained thru mystic contemplation, naturally the intelligent man will be inclined to turn his back on the world and devote himself to a more or less hermit-like existence. There are, moreover, very special reasons for asceticism. Actions lead to rebirth; so inaction, or the nearest possible approach to it, withdrawal from the world, is desirable. Furthermore, as we have seen, desires are the root of evil, because they enchain man to the things of this life, and distract his attention from his true goal. He must, therefore, seek to overcome his desires. One way of doing this is to avoid the objects of desire as much as possible, by living a solitary life, preferably in the wilderness. Another way is by positive acts of self-repression, even self-torture, to "mortify the flesh" and reduce it to subjection. Another is by means of self-hypnosis to induce a state of trance, or half-trance, in which one may attain nearly complete, if only temporary, freedom from the distractions of the world, and a sort of approach to the "unconscious consciousness" of union with the One. All of these varying forms of ascetic austerities have been more or less practised by many Hindu sects, sometimes in very extreme forms. They are all suggested by the expression *tapas*, "heat, fervor," as it is used in the Upaniṣads and later. As so used the word contains both a physical and a "spiritual" connotation. Physical, in that many ascetics engaged in often very strenuous exertions, or deliberately subjected themselves to the heat of the sun and of fire, to subdue their physical passions. "Spiritual," in that their theoretical aim, at least, was always to produce the desired religious fervor or ecstasy thru which they hoped to gain enlightenment. In theory, all such practices were only a means, the end being enlightenment. They prepared the soul for this end by subduing desires and inducing a spiritual attitude favorable to the reception of enlightenment. But in this case, too, as in the case of the theory of divine grace and devotion to the Deity, the means became the end in some later sects, which came to think of salvation as resulting directly from asceticism, not from enlightenment brought on by asceticism There are sects which teach that salvation is sure to come to one who starves himself to death — the *ne plus ultra* of ascetic practice. This extreme, however, is exceptional.[31]

[31] In popular belief ascetic practices came to be regarded as a means of acquiring all sorts of supernatural or magic powers; just as knowledge (the acquisition of which

We see, then, that the word *tapas*, "fervor," had both a physical and a "spiritual" aspect in both the early Vedic speculations and their later successors, but that there was a change in the connotation on each side. The Upaniṣads took up the early word for "fervor" or "warmth" and reinterpreted it in terms of their own views. Common to both periods is the use of the primarily physical term to characterize a certain type of religious life, tho a different type in each period. The early use of the term in cosmogonic connections may also be presumed to have contributed to the use of it in the Upaniṣads as a tentative definition of the First Principle, or a means of knowing it. ("Seek to know the *brahman* by fervor [austerity, *tapas*]; *brahman* is fervor [austerity]!")[32] Not a few Upaniṣad passages speak of attaining the *ātman* thru *tapas*, either alone or in conjunction with other potencies. For them, however, it remains a subordinate matter, on the whole. The sentence just quoted is not at all typical of their general attitude. In this respect the Bhagavad Gītā agrees with them. Indeed, the usual attitude of the Gītā is definitely opposed to asceticism; it seeks to justify participation in normal, worldly life, tho with qualification. Only rarely does it speak in terms which seem to recommend withdrawal from the world.[33]

To summarize this chapter: the Upaniṣads show us the beginnings of the fundamental principles of later, classical Hinduism. These may be grouped under three general headings. First, pessimism: all ordinary life is evil. Second, transmigration, with the doctrine of karma: living souls are subject to an indefinite series of lives, all more or less like this life, the condition of the individual in each being determined by his moral conduct in previous existences. Third, salvation: the only hope for release from this endless chain of evil existences is (primarily) by "knowledge," that is, intuitive realization of the supreme metaphysical truth; as preparations or aids to the attainment of this knowledge are recognized morality, devotion to a supreme personality, and ascetic austerities, altho all of these are usually kept in a quite subordinate position in the Upaniṣads. In various later sects one or another of them at times assumes such importance as to obscure the original means of salvation, "knowledge." Except in this last respect, virtually all Hindu sects and philosophies agree regarding these basic postulates, however much they may differ on other matters.

was the theoretical object of ascetic practices) was understood by the vulgar in terms of magic power. Some of the later systems of philosophy which attach great importance to austerities are not free from this degradation of the principle.

[32] Taittirīya Upaniṣad, 3.2 ff.

[33] See Chapter VII.

CHAPTER IV

Prehistory of the God of the Bhagavad Gītā

It could hardly be expected that the popular interest would be gripped by Upaniṣadic thought. It was too speculative, too abstract, to appeal to any but a small proportion of the population. The great mass of mankind demanded, as always, a personal, quasi-human god or gods to worship; it could not be satisfied by mystic contemplation of a nameless Soul, even if it be the Soul of the universe. Some more acceptable outlet for the religious feeling of the people had to be provided; and there is good reason to believe that it was provided. Unfortunately, the evidence about it is mostly indirect and secondary. We can judge of it, for the most part, only from its traces in such later works as the Bhagavad Gītā, which clearly presuppose a considerable development of popular religion, distinct from the higher thought of the Upaniṣads but contemporary therewith. In the Gītā these two streams are blended. We have no records that show us the popular beliefs of that period in a pure form.

For this reason, it is scarcely possible to attempt any extensive reconstruction of those popular beliefs. The principal thing to be said about them is that they were certainly theistic, and presumably tended towards a monotheism, of a more or less qualified sort. That is, presumably various local or tribal deities were worshipped in different parts of India, each occupying a position somewhat similar to that of Yahweh among the Jews — each being regarded as the chief or perhaps the sole god of his people or tribe, tho the existence of the gods of other tribes was not denied. These local deities were, we may assume, of very different types and origins. Sometimes they may have been old gods of aboriginal, non-Aryan tribes. Sometimes they seem to have been local heroes, deified after death.

Such a local deity must have been the Kṛṣṇa who appears as the Supreme Deity, the "Blessed One," in the Bhagavad Gītā. He was apparently a deified local chieftain, the head of the Vṛṣṇi clan. Indeed, he appears as such, in strictly human guise, in the greater part of the Mahābhārata. In the Gītā he is still both god and man; an incarnation of the Deity in human form. We know nothing of the process by which he attained divine honors, nor of his earlier history as a god, before the Bhagavad Gītā, which is probably the earliest work preserved to us in which he appears as such. In this work he has all the attributes of a full-fledged monotheistic deity, and at the same time, as we shall see, the attributes of the Upaniṣadic Absolute. In other words, the popular God is philosophized into a figure who can appeal to both the higher and the lower circles of the population. Therein lies the strength of Kṛṣṇaism in later India; it is many-sided enough to satisfy the religious requirements of almost any man, whatever his intellectual or social status may be.

The Upaniṣads themselves are not entirely free from quasi-monotheistic touches, some of which may perhaps be interpreted as concessions to this same popular demand for a personal god. Especially interesting, and important for later Hinduism, is the personalization of the philosophic term Brahman, as a name for the Absolute, which appears even in some of the earliest Upaniṣads. The word *brahman* is primarily and originally neuter in gender, and remains so usually thruout the Upaniṣads and the Bhagavad Gītā; but occasionally it acquires a personality, as a sort of creating and ruling deity, and then it has masculine gender. It thus becomes the god Brahmā, familiar to later Hinduism as the nominal head of the Triad consisting of Brahmā the Creator, Viṣṇu the Preserver, and Śiva the Destroyer. This trinity appears only in comparatively late Upaniṣads, and no clear mention of it is found in the Bhagavad Gītā, altho the Gītā at least once refers to the masculine and personal Brahmā, "the Lord sitting on the lotus-seat."[1] But this grammatical trick was not sufficient to satisfy the craving of the men of India. Even masculinized, Brahman-Brahmā remained too bloodless to attract many worshipers. Later Hinduism pays lip-homage to him, but reserves its real worship for his colleagues, Viṣṇu and Śiva.

Viṣṇu and Śiva, under various names and forms, are the real gods of later India. Śiva-worship, tho certainly much older than the Bhagavad Gītā, hardly appears therein,[2] and may therefore be left out of consideration in this book. But we must say a few words about Viṣṇu, since he was identified with Kṛṣṇa, the Gītā's God, or regarded as incarnate in Him. This identification seems to me to appear clearly in the Gītā itself.[3]

Viṣṇu was one of the gods of the Rig Veda, and probably, like most of them, a nature-god. He seems to have been a personification of the sun. But the Rig Veda contains a number of sun-gods (perhaps originally belonging to different tribes, or else representing different aspects of the sun's power). Viṣṇu is one of the less prominent and less important ones. He is distinctly a minor figure in the Rig Veda. We hear that he measures the universe in three great strides, which refer figuratively to the sun's progress

[1] xi. 15.

[2] Śiva, under various of his innumerable names, is however mentioned (e.g. x. 23).

[3] A distinguished Hindu scholar, the late Sir R. G. Bhandarkar, thought that Kṛṣṇa was not yet identified with Viṣṇu in the Gītā, tho he was soon afterwards. See his *Vaiṣṇavism, Śaivism and Minor Religious Systems*, page 13. But Kṛṣṇa is directly addressed as Viṣṇu in xi. 24 and 30; and I do not believe that Viṣṇu can here mean "the sun."

across the sky. The third stride lands him in "the highest foot-step (or, place; the word has both meanings) of Viṣṇu," which means the zenith. This is thought of as the highest point in the universe, and at times it is described as a kind of solar paradise, to which the spirits of the blessed dead may go. So in post-Rig-Vedic literature, we hear expressions of the desire for attaining "Viṣṇu's highest place." So, also, in this period, Viṣṇu is occasionally declared to be "the highest of the gods"; this is doubtless to be understood in a literal, physical sense, because Viṣṇu's abode is the "top of the world." In the same period, we find very frequently the statement that "Viṣṇu is the sacrifice." Why he should have been singled out for this honor, we cannot tell; there are other gods whose far greater prominence would seem to us to give them a better claim to be regarded as a personification of the ritual. But the frequency of the statement leaves no room for doubt that the priests of the "Middle Vedic" (Brāhmaṇa) period generally regarded Viṣṇu in this way. And since, as we have seen, to them the "sacrifice" was the central power of the universe, we see that from their point of view no higher compliment was possible. Evidently Viṣṇu was acquiring a much more dignified position than he had in the Rig Veda.

The Upaniṣads add nothing to the history of Viṣṇu. They — that is, the older ones, those which antedate the Gītā — mention his name only three or four times, and quite in the style of the Middle-Vedic period. But suddenly, in the Gītā and other contemporary writings, we find Viṣṇu recognized as a supreme monotheistic deity, worshiped either under his own name, or in the form of various incarnations, the chief of which is Kṛṣṇa. This was at a time when the Vedic religion, as a whole, was nearly dead. Its gods no longer had a real hold on any class of the people. Their existence was not denied, but they were reduced to the rank of petty spirits. Even the once all-important sacrifices were largely falling into disuse. But if the ritual religion was perishing, the priestly class was not. By this time it was recognized as a definite and hereditary caste, the brahmanhood, which claimed the headship of human society. With this fact, probably, is to be connected the identification of the god or hero Kṛṣṇa, and other popular gods and heroes, with the old Vedic god Viṣṇu. Thus a sacerdotal tinge was given to the thriving monotheism which had such a hold on the mass of the people. Brahmanism stooped to conquer; it absorbed popular cults which it had not the strength to uproot. The simple and ancient device of identification of one god with another furnished the means to this end.

It remains something of a mystery to scholars why Viṣṇu, rather than some other Vedic deity, was selected for this purpose. Even after the development described in the last paragraph but one, Viṣṇu is by no means the most prominent god of the pantheon. Many steps in the long process have evidently disappeared from our sight. But probably his frequent identification with the sacrifice, and his growing eschatological importance as the ruler of a kind of paradise for the dead in his "highest place," have something to do with it.

We have, then, finally, a union of at least three strands in the monotheistic deity of the Bhagavad Gītā: a popular god-hero of a local tribe, an ancient Vedic deity belonging to the hieratic ritual religion, and the philosophic Absolute of the Upaniṣads. The blend is, as we shall see, by no means perfect. Especially the monistic, Upaniṣadic element is sometimes rather clearly distinguished from the theistic element or elements; the author of the Gītā himself underlines this distinction at times.[4] But for the most part it is hard to disentangle one from the other.

[4] See Chapter VI, p. 150.

INTERPRETATION OF THE BHAGAVAD GĪTĀ

SECOND PART

THE TEACHINGS OF THE BHAGAVAD GĪTĀ

CHAPTER V

Soul and Body

We saw that the Upaniṣads center their attention on a search for the central, fundamental, and animating principle of the universe, and of man; that these two objects of speculation are regarded in them as parallel, the universal macrocosm being compared to the human microcosm; and that this parallelism indeed turns into an identity, which results in an equation between the "soul" or real self of man and that of the universe. So frequent and striking are such expressions in the Upaniṣads that this is often, tho I think not without exaggeration, regarded as the prime motif of Upaniṣadic thought. It is "knowledge" of this mystic truth which makes man omnipotent, makes him master of the universe, and so "free"; free, that is, from the limitations and annoyances of finite life.

In spite of the fact that the Bhagavad Gītā is saturated with the atmosphere of the Upaniṣads, this doctrine of theirs is not exactly prominent in it. It is not unknown to it; several passages in which it speaks of the human soul come very close to that view.[1] It would indeed be strange if it had avoided it altogether. It is curious enough that it has so nearly suppressed it, in view of its obvious debt to Upaniṣadic thought. The chief reason for the suppression probably lay in the fact that this monistic view was not easy to reconcile with the ardent, devotional theism of the Gītā. Even tho, as we shall see, the Gītā regards God as immanent in all beings, and its author hopes for ultimate union with Him, still he seems to shrink from the bold assertion "I am God," which requires more courage than the Upaniṣadic "I am Brahman," simply because Brahman is impersonal and the Gītā's God is definitely personal. Union with God is projected into the future, and is not put on a basis of equality between the soul and God.[2] Once the Gītā speaks of the human soul as a *part* of God.[3] Generally God is a personality distinct from the human soul, and superior to it.

[1] ii. 17: "But know thou that That One (the human soul is referred to) by which all this universe is pervaded is indestructible. Of this imperishable one no one can cause the destruction." — ii. 24: "Eternal, omnipresent, fixed, immovable, everlasting is He (the human soul)." — xiii. 27: "Abiding alike in all beings, the supreme Lord (the human soul), not perishing when they (the beings) perish, — who sees him, he (truly) sees."

[2] Some of the Christian mystics seem more courageous. Compare Angelus Silesius's

"Ich bin so gross wie Gott,
Er ist wie ich so klein."

[3] xv. 7: "A part just of Me, becoming the eternal soul in living beings," etc.

The Upaniṣadic notion of the human soul is, however, clearly retained in the Gītā as far as concerns its individual nature. It is still the essential part of man, that which does not perish at death. Indeed, the dignity and importance of the soul is brought out if possible even more strongly than is usual in the Upaniṣads, in one respect; namely, in the contrast that is emphasized between the soul and what is not soul. This contrast is rather a minor matter in most of the Upaniṣads. They are so charmed by the contemplation of the soul, which they find in everything, that they virtually ignore the existence of everything that is not soul,[4] or else brush it aside with the summary remark that "whatever is other than that (the soul) is evil."[5] At any rate, most of them are not enough interested in the non-soul to speculate much about its nature. The Gītā, on the other hand, has definite theories about the structure of the non-soul or body, — largely inherited, to be sure, from older times, and to some extent hinted at in certain of the Upaniṣads These are used to contrast the body with the soul; and the comparison, of course, is much to the advantage of the soul. Thus in the opening part of the dialog, Kṛṣṇa instructs Arjuna that he should not grieve for the soul, because it is immortal, and inaccessible to the sufferings which afflict the body. "It is declared that these bodies come to an end; but the Embodied (Soul) in them is eternal, indestructible, unfathomable."[6] "He (the soul) is not born, nor does he ever die; nor, once being, shall he evermore cease to be. Unborn, eternal, everlasting from oldest times, he is not slain when the body is slain."[7]

We find, in fact, that the Gītā's most usual and characteristic position is definitely dualistic. There are two eternal principles, eternally distinct from each other: "soul" (usually called *puruṣa*, "man, person, spirit"; sometimes *ātman*, "self"; other synonyms also occur), and what may perhaps be called "non-soul" rather than "body," since, as we shall see presently, it includes what are among us commonly regarded as "mental" faculties; the usual Hindu term is *prakṛti*, "nature, material nature, matter." The soul is absolutely unitary, undifferentiated, and without qualities; not

[4] Some scholars say that they even *deny* the real existence of anything other than the soul, as certain schools of the later Vedānta philosophy do. I do not agree with this view.

[5] Bṛhad Āraṇyaka Upaniṣad, 3.4.2.

[6] ii. 18.

[7] ii. 20. Compare also ii. 11, 25, 30. It is painful to have to add that this doctrine is here applied to a justification of war, and of killing in general; since the soul cannot be killed, and the body does not matter (and since, moreover, it must die in any case, ii. 26, 27), "therefore fight," says Kṛṣṇa (ii. 18). A charitable explanation would be that this is a concession to the dramatic situation of the poem, as inserted in the Mahābhārata; and this could be supported by various texts in the Gītā which are distinctly hostile to violence. But we shall see that there are other ethical, as well as metaphysical, inconsistencies in the Gītā. See Chapter XI.

subject to any change or alteration, and not participating in any action. Material nature, or the non-soul, is what performs all acts. It assumes manifold forms, and is constantly subject to change — evolution, devolution, and variation.

The variety of material nature is expressed in two ways. First, it is composed of three elements called *guṇas*, that is, "threads, strands," or "qualities":[8] namely, *sattva*, "goodness, purity"; *rajas*, "passion, activity"; and *tamas*, "darkness, dullness, inactivity." Mingled in varying proportions, these three "strands" or qualities make up all matter. Preponderance of one or another of them determines the character of any given part of material nature.[9] But material nature includes what with us are often called the "mental" faculties of living beings, particularly of man. This is made clear in one passage in the Gītā,[10] where we find a second and much more elaborate statement of the constituents of material nature — or rather, this time, of its evolvents; for, tho this is not clearly stated here, it is obvious that we are dealing with an evolutionary theory which is very familiar in contemporary and later Hindu philosophy. According to this, out of the primal, undifferentiated "matter" develops first the faculty of consciousness or will (the term, *buddhi*, approximately covers both of these English terms); then the "I-faculty," the organ of self-consciousness (*ahaṃkāra*); then the thought-organ (*manas*, sometimes etymologically translated "mind"), which mediates between sense-perception and the self-consciousness, and is regarded as the function of a special, "inner" sense-organ; with it the faculties of the ten sense-organs,[11] five intellectual (of sight, smell, hearing, taste and feeling) and five organs of action (of speech [function of the speech-organs], grasping [of the hands], locomotion [of the feet], evacua-

[8] The word is probably both concrete and abstract in the Gītā; the *guṇas* are both material "constituent elements," like strands of a rope, and qualifying characteristics. No clear distinction was made at this time between these two things (cf. Oldenberg, *Upanishaden und Buddhismus*, 1st ed., p. 217 f.; 2d ed., p. 188 f.). The later Sāṃkhya philosophy insists that the *guṇas* are physical, constituent parts of matter, not what we call qualities. And this certainly fits the primary and literal meaning of the word *guṇa*, "strand (of a rope)." Yet its figurative meaning of "quality" is also very familiar in the Gītā's time.

[9] The results of the preponderance of each of the three "strands" in various parts of *prakṛti* are set forth in some detail in the Gītā, xiv. 5–18, and the whole of chapter xvii. Generally speaking, the theory is that the best and highest forms of matter or nature are those in which *sattva*, "goodness, purity," predominates; in the worst and lowest forms *tamas*, "darkness, dullness," predominates; the predominance of *rajas*, "activity" or "passion," is found in a large variety of forms whose ethical values are mostly intermediate or indeterminate.

[10] xiii. 5, 6.

[11] The Gītā seems to include both the physical organs and their functions in the same verbal expressions. I shall not here discuss the later Hindu usage.

tion, and generation); also the five "subtle elements," the abstract essences of the material objects (or as we say, reversing the direction, stimulants) of the five senses (sound, as the object of hearing, etc.); and finally the five gross elements, earth, air, fire, water, and ether.[12] All of these forms of material nature — twenty-four in all, including the "undifferentiated" form — are alike composed of the three above-mentioned "strands" (*guṇas*), in varying proportions. It will be seen that the two classifications are not inconsistent, but cross one another, the one being, so to speak, vertical, the other horizontal.

It is, as I have said, only "material nature" or "matter" that acts. "Actions are performed entirely by the strands (*guṇas*) of material nature. He whose soul is deluded by the I-faculty imagines that he is the doer." [13] That is, owing to the confusion created by the activity of the organ of self-consciousness — *which is part of matter, not of the soul* — one imagines that "he" himself (his soul, his real self, or *ātman*) performs actions. "But he who knows the truth of the separation (of the soul, on the one hand, from both) the strands (of matter) and action (on the other), knowing that (in any action) it is (not the soul that acts but) the strands of matter that act upon the strands, is not enthralled." [14] "And who sees that acts are exclusively performed by material nature alone, and likewise that his soul does nothing, he (truly) sees." [15] "The disciplined man who knows the truth shall think: 'I am not doing anything at all,' whether he be seeing, hearing, touching, smelling, eating, walking, sleeping, breathing, speaking, evacuating, grasping, opening or closing his eyes; he holds fast to the thought that it is the (material) senses that are operating on the objects of sense." [16] "When the Beholder (the soul) perceives that no other than the strands (of matter) acts and knows that which is above the strands, he goes unto My estate." [17]

What, then, is the function of the soul? As the passage last quoted indicates, it "beholds" the activities of matter, passively, and without participation. "Passively" in the sense that it has no relation to those activities at all; not in the sense that it is affected by them, for its true, fundamental nature is just as free from the effects of action as from its performance. "The Lord (the soul) does not receive (i.e., reap the fruit of)

[12] I shall refrain from describing the precise stages of this evolutionary process as set forth in the later Sāṃkhya philosophy. It is not clear to what extent they had been formulated in the time of the Gītā. One verse of the Gītā (iii. 42) lists a few of these "evolvents" in climactic order, but without asserting any genetic relationship, — in fact, perhaps implying rather that none exists, since the "highest" member of the series is there the Soul, which is elsewhere clearly stated to be unrelated to matter.

[13] iii. 27.

[14] iii. 28.

[15] xiii. 29.

[16] v. 8, 9.

[17] xiv. 19.

any one's sin, nor yet (of) his good deeds."[18] "Swords cut him not, fire burns him not, water wets him not, wind dries him not. He cannot be cut, he cannot be burnt, he cannot be wet, nor yet dried. Eternal, omnipresent, fixed, immovable, everlasting is he (the human soul)."[19] Elsewhere the soul is called the "knower" of matter: "This body is called the Field. He who knows it (i.e., the soul), him those who know the truth call the Field-knower."[20] The soul, then, merely looks on and "knows" matter and its acts, but has no real connection with them.

And yet, inconsistently as it seems at first sight, the soul is spoken of as experiencing pleasure and pain, which result from material contacts and processes. "Know that both material nature and the soul are eternal; know that both the modifications (or 'evolvents,' viz. will, I-faculty, organ of thought and other sense-organs, and subtle and gross elements) and the strands (*guṇas*) spring from material nature. Material nature is declared to be the cause of effects, instrumentality, and agency; the soul is declared to be the cause of enjoyment (i.e., experiencing) of pleasure and pain. For the soul, residing in material nature, enjoys the strands (*guṇas*) that are born of material nature. Its attachment to the strands is the reason for its various births in good and evil stations."[21] The key to the seeming inconsistency (which is really due to a certain laxity or inaccuracy in the passage just quoted) is indicated in the last sentence, the thought of which is more fully expressed in another passage, where it is said that the soul "draws (to itself) the (five) senses, with the organ of thought as the sixth, which rest in material nature. . . . Making use of hearing, sight, touch, taste, and smell, and the organ of thought (all of which are really material), it pursues the objects of sense. Fools do not perceive that it (the soul) is attended by the strands (*guṇas*, of matter) when it is passing out or remaining fixed (in the body) or enjoying (experiencing, viz. the objects of sense). Those whose eye is knowledge see this."[22] It is only because the soul is associated with matter that it "enjoys," or rather (it would be more accurate to say) *seems* to "enjoy," material processes. "Those who are deluded by the strands (*guṇas*) of material nature are enthralled in the actions of the strands."[23] In other words, it is, strictly speaking, not the soul that "enjoys" — experiences — anything. That it seems to do so is due to the confusion caused by the organ of self-consciousness, the "I-faculty," which is a product of material nature and really quite disconnected with the soul, and from which in turn spring all the sense-organs and their objects. Were it not for this, the soul would perceive that it has no relation whatever to the activities and sufferings of matter. Since to the Gītā the general Hindu

[18] v. 15.
[19] ii. 23, 24
[20] xiii. 1.
[21] xiii. 19–21.
[22] xv. 7–10.
[23] iii. 29.

pessimistic view of life is axiomatic, it follows that this "enjoyment" is in reality naught but evil and suffering, and that the association of the soul with matter is a bondage. "Goodness (*sattva*), activity (passion, *rajas*) and darkness (*tamas*), — these strands, springing from material nature, bind in the body the immortal soul." [24] It is only the unenlightened man whom they *can* bind. When one attains true enlightenment, that is, realization of the true nature of the soul and matter and their fundamental independence of each other, then, by virtue of this perfect, mystic knowledge, he obtains release; his soul transcends matter and is freed from it for good and all, and he is freed from the chain of rebirths. "Who thus understands the soul and material nature together with the strands (of the latter), — in whatever state he may be, he is not (to be) born again." [25] "The Embodied (Soul), transcending these three strands (of matter) that spring from the body, freed from birth, death, old age, and sorrow, attains immortality (here a poetic expression for *nirvāṇa*)." [26] "Mentally abandoning all actions (that is, taking no interest in any action which the body may perform), the Embodied (Soul) sits at peace, in control, in his nine-doored citadel (the body), and neither acts nor causes action at all." [27]

Note that this is a distinctly anthropomorphic dualism. As we have already seen, it is characteristic of Hindu speculation that it thinks of the whole universe in human terms; this was particularly true of the Upaniṣads, and remains true, generally speaking, of all later systems. This attitude assumes various forms. The Gītā says: "All creatures whatsoever, motionless (inanimate objects and plants) or moving (animals), are produced by the union of the Field (material nature) and the Field-knower (the soul)." [28] This seems to attribute to all nature not only "mental" faculties, will, self-consciousness, and thinking organ, which are parts of material nature and its primary evolvents, but also a soul that is distinct from material nature. Some Hindu sects — particularly the Jains — clearly and definitely accept the extreme implications of this theory, and believe that even inanimate objects are inhabited by souls, which are subject to transmigration like animal souls. Other Hindu systems do not carry it as far as that, at least in definite statements. But to all of them man is the only part of the universe that really counts. Animals (usually plants also) are to them potential humans; and the rest of the world they virtually ignore in their speculations. We need not consider here the extreme idealistic monism of Śaṃkara's Vedānta

[24] xiv. 5.

[25] xiii. 23.

[26] xiv. 20.

[27] v. 13. We shall have more to say of the various means of salvation found in the Gītā in Chapters VIII and IX.

[28] xiii. 26.

philosophy, according to which there is only One that truly exists, namely Brahman, the world soul, with which the human soul is really identical; all else is illusion (*māyā*), existing only in appearance, as a mirage, and not in reality. This system developed long after the Gītā, as it seems to me, altho it claims to be founded on the Upaniṣads. In a sense it is founded on them; it is only the logical conclusion, or extreme application, of their doctrine that the essential part of man is one with the essential part of the universe. But the Upaniṣads did not say "the non-soul does not exist." They only tended to ignore its existence or its importance — to wave it aside as unworthy of their consideration; they were not interested in it. This explains why the Upaniṣads could be made the basis for such diametrically opposite systems as the monism of Śaṃkara's Vedānta on the one hand and the Gītā's dualism on the other. The latter was reduced to more systematic forms by the later Sāṃkhya and Yoga philosophies, both of which recognize the reality and independence of soul and matter. They differ on the existence of God, which is accepted by the Yoga but denied by the Sāṃkhya.[29] The Gītā agrees with the Yoga in this respect. All of these views derive from the Upaniṣadic speculations centering about the human soul; and all agree that the non-soul, or material nature, is something from which the soul should utterly detach itself, whether it really exists (Gītā, Sāṃkhya, and Yoga) or is merely illusory (Śaṃkara's Vedānta).

[29] Or rather by certain representatives of the later Sāṃkhya, which have been, a little hastily, taken as typical of the whole school. As a matter of fact, a theistic Sāṃkhya has probably always existed, and was certainly known late as well as early.

CHAPTER VI

The Nature of God

We have spoken of the metaphysics of the Gītā as dualistic, as recognizing two fundamental principles, the soul and the non-soul (body, or material nature). But it is impossible to read far in the Gītā without finding that this description does not fully represent its author's metaphysics, at least in his most typical mood. It leaves out of account his idea of God, which is as it were superimposed upon the dualistic system outlined in the last chapter.

How does God fit into this system? Is He a sort of third principle, higher than the other two and distinct from them? So we are told at times, perhaps most clearly in the following passage: "There are two spirits [1] here in the world, a perishable and an imperishable one. The perishable (i.e., material nature) is all beings. The imperishable (i.e., the soul, spirit) is called the immovable (unchangeable). But there is another, a supreme Spirit, called the Highest Soul (Paramātman), the Eternal Lord who enters into the three worlds and supports them." [2] Here the Supreme Soul, God, is definitely set off against the individual soul and matter, as a third principle. Somewhat similarly in another passage, we first have a statement of the ordinary dualism: "This body is called the Field; him who knows it (the soul) those who know the truth call the Field-knower" — which is immediately followed by this: "Know that I (God) am the Field-knower in all Fields." [3]

But even in these very passages let it be noted that God, tho in a sense something other than either material nature or the individual souls of men, is at the same time regarded as immanent in them. "Whoso sees Me in all and all in Me, for him I am not lost, and he is not lost for Me. Whoso, attaining to (belief in) oneness, reveres Me as located in all beings, he, the disciplined, tho he may abide in any possible state, abides in Me." [4] "Attaining to (belief in) *oneness*!" Thus thru its God the Gītā seems after all

[1] The word used is *puruṣa*, literally "man," which elsewhere means strictly "soul" and is not applied to the body or material nature; yet here the "perishable spirit" can obviously mean nothing but *prakṛti*, material nature. This is an example of the loose language of the Gītā which often reminds us that we are reading a mystic poem, not a logical treatise on metaphysics.

[2] xv. 16, 17.

[3] xiii. 1,2.

[4] vi. 30, 31.

to arrive at an ultimate monism. The essential part, the fundamental element, in every thing, is after all One — is God. "There is nothing else that is higher than I (beyond, outside of Me); on Me this All is strung like necklaces of pearls on a string."[5] "Also the seed of all beings, that am I. There is no being, moving or motionless, that is without Me."[6] "I am taste in water, the light in the moon and sun, the sacred syllable Om in all the Vedas, sound in the ether, manliness in men. The goodly odor in the earth am I, and brilliance in the fire; I am life in all beings, and austerity in ascetics. Know Me as the eternal seed of all creatures. I am the intelligence of the intelligent, the majesty of the majestic."[7] God is the animating principle in everything; it is He that "makes the wheels" of the universe "go 'round," that acts in all natural activities and processes: "The Lord abides in the heart of all beings and makes all beings go around by His mysterious power (*māyā*), as if they were fixed on a (revolving) machine (that is, probably, like puppets in a puppet-play)."[8] "The splendor of the sun that illumines the whole world and the splendor that is in the moon and in fire, know that to be My splendor. Entering into the earth I support (all) beings by My power; becoming the juicy soma I make all plants to grow. Becoming fire (as the principle of digestion, regarded by the Hindus as a 'cooking' by bodily heat) I enter into the bodies of animate creatures, and, joining with the upper and nether breaths, I digest their food of all four sorts. I have entered into the heart of every man; from Me come memory, knowledge, and disputation (in reasoning). I alone am the object of the (sacred) knowledge of all the Vedas; I am the author of the Vedānta (the Upaniṣads, the summation of the esoteric doctrines of the Vedas), and I too am the sole knower of the Veda."[9] So, of course, God is repeatedly declared to be the Creator, Supporter, Ruler of all that is; the origin and dissolution of the universe,[10] "both death that carries off all and the origin of creatures that are to be,"[11] "both immortality and death, both the existent and the non-existent,"[12] "the beginning and the middle and the end of beings."[13]

Such words lead to the question of the existence of evil and how to reconcile it with the belief in an all-embracing God. Every theistic religion has its difficulties with the problem of evil. In describing the manifestations of God in the universe, the Gītā, quite naturally, tends to emphasize the good side of things; but at times it does not shrink from including the evil also. Since *all* comes from God, it seems impossible to deny that origin to anything. "Whatsoever states of being there are, be they of the nature of goodness, passion, or darkness (the three *guṇas* or strands of matter, as set forth in the last chapter), know that all of them come from Me

[5] vii. 7.
[6] x. 39.
[7] vii. 8–10.
[8] xviii. 61.
[9] xv. 12–15.
[10] vii. 6.
[11] x. 34.
[12] ix. 19.
[13] x. 20, x. 32.

alone."[14] In another passage, God is declared the source of all "psychic" states and experiences, *good and bad alike*, tho the good predominate in the list: "Enlightenment, knowledge, freedom from delusion, patience, truth, self-control, peace, pleasure, *pain*, coming-into-being, passing away, *fear*, and fearlessness too; harmlessness, indifference (equanimity), content, austerity, generosity, fame, and *disrepute* — the states of creatures, of all various sorts, come from Me alone."[15] More definite recognition of the origin even of evil in God is found in this: "I am the gambling of rogues, the majesty of the majestic; I am conquest, I am adventure (of conquerors and adventurers); I am the courage of the courageous. . . . I am the violence of conquerors, I am the statecraft of ambitious princes; I too am the taciturnity of things that are secret, I am the knowledge of the learned."[16]

If even in these passages we seem to find a tendency to slur over the evil of the world and its necessary relation to a quasi-pantheistic God, in other places the Gītā feels it necessary to qualify its semipantheism by definitely ruling out evil from God's nature. Thus to a passage in the seventh chapter which is strongly suggestive of pantheism, and which I quoted on the preceding page — "I am taste in water, etc.; I am the intelligence of the intelligent, the majesty of the majestic" — there is added this significant verse: "I am the strength of the strong, *free from lust and passion*; I am desire in (all) beings (but) *not* (such desire as is) *opposed to righteousness*."[17] Thus the Gītā strengthens its appeal to the natural man, or to "common sense," at the expense of logic and consistency.

This stricture (if it be considered a stricture) seems to me not unfair, even tho I doubt whether it can be said that the Gītā ever commits itself to absolute pantheism. It undoubtedly comes very close to it, as in some of the passages I have quoted. That God is *in* all, or all in God, it frequently says; and hence we may fairly ask whether God is also in that which is evil (or it in Him). But this is not exactly saying that God *is* all, that God is identical with all and all with God, there being no remainder on either side. Such a definitely pantheistic statement is not, I think, to be found in the Gītā. Certainly we find many expressions which seem to deny it. And that in two ways. In the first place, God's nature may be limited by the exclusion of certain parts of the universe or forms of existence. And secondly, God is spoken of as extending beyond the universe, as including more than "all beings."

As to the first point, the word "limited" as applied to God's nature is my own, and would undoubtedly have been strenuously repudiated by the author of the Gītā. He would have said — indeed he does say again and again, in many different ways — that God is limitless, that He includes *all*

[14] vii. 12.
[15] x. 4, 5.
[16] x. 36, 38.
[17] vii. 11.

forms. Yet we have seen that at times he feels compelled to deny that God manifests Himself in certain forms of existence which are felt as morally evil; altho at other times he swallows even this dose. Whatever terminology one uses, the fact remains that the Gītā repeatedly manifests a tendency to find God only in the best or highest forms of existence. The worse and lower forms are at least implicitly left out. This tendency is so natural as to be almost inevitable in a writer who is, after all, pervaded by a spirit of ardent, personal theism — however tinged with quasi-pantheism. Philosophically, the doctrine that God is *in* all leaves a loophole which can be stretched to admit a good deal. God is the soul, the essential part of everything; this may be interpreted as meaning the highest or noblest part of everything. Now lay the emphasis on the word *part*, and the trick is turned. Any entity may be regarded as a part of some larger whole, just as any entity (except perhaps, for the time being at least, the modern proton and neutron) may be treated as a compound whole and analyzed into parts. By choosing your "whole" and making it sufficiently inclusive, God can be found in some "part" of every "whole," and yet excused from responsibility for anything that would seem unworthy of Him. Such a background seems needed to account for such passages as the long series of verses found in the tenth chapter,[18] in which God is identified with (*only!*) the first, highest, or best, of every conceivable class of beings: "Of lights I am the sun . . . of stars the moon, of Vedas the Sāma Veda, of gods Indra (the king of the old Vedic gods), of sense-organs the thought-organ . . . of mountains Mount Meru," and so forth indefinitely.

On the other hand, the Gītā's theism differs from pantheism also in that it regards God as *more* than the universe. "Whatsoever creature possesses lordliness or majesty or greatness, know thou that every such creature springs from a *fraction* of My glory. . . . With *one part* of Myself I remain the support of this entire universe." [19] "I am not in them (all beings); they are in Me." [20] "By Me all this world is permeated, by Me whose form is unmanifest. All beings rest in Me; and I do not rest in them." [21] In the next verse after this last, the author retracts even this statement; it is too much to say even that the world is in God: "And (yet) beings do not rest in Me; behold My divine mystery! My self is the support of beings, and does not rest in beings; it is the cause of being of beings." [22] The dictum that the First Principle is more than all existing things, that the universe is only a *part* thereof, is at least as old as the "Puruṣa" hymn of the Rig Veda,[23] in which the entire universe is derived from only one-quarter of the cosmic Purusa or "Person."

[18] x. 21–37.
[19] x. 41, 42.
[20] vii. 12.
[21] ix. 4.
[22] ix. 5.
[23] RV. 10.90.3, 4.

This is by no means the only point in which the Gītā's picture of God shows relations with older formulas for the First Principle. While, as we have seen, the older speculations, so far as we know them, tend to impersonal and non-theistic formulations of the One, still many of the expressions which they use in describing that One can quite well be applied to a personal God; and they and similar expressions are so applied in the Gītā. Many of the Gītā's descriptions of God sound as if they were taken bodily from the Upaniṣads. Thus: "Thou art the Supreme Brahman, the Supreme Station (or Light), the Supreme Purifier; the eternal Puruṣa ('Person,' Spirit), the divine, the Primal God, the Unborn Lord."[24] "The ancient Seer, the Governor, finer than an atom . . . the Establisher of all, whose form is unthinkable, the Sun-colored, who is beyond darkness."[25] "I am the father of this world, the mother, the establisher, the ancestor. . . . The goal, supporter, lord, witness, dwelling-place, refuge, friend; the origin, dissolution, maintenance, treasure-house, the eternal seed (of all)."[26] The term Brahman, favorite expression in the Upaniṣads for the Absolute, is frequently found in the Gītā; and often it is hard to say whether the author means to identify Brahman with God or not. The fact doubtless is that, as set forth in Chapter IV, the Upaniṣadic Brahman has contributed largely to the Gītā's notion of God, which has absorbed it along with other, more theistic elements. As a rule, no clear distinction is made between them. But in one or two places the Gītā shows a realization of a possible difference of opinion as to whether the Supreme is personal or impersonal. And, most interestingly, it definitely recognizes *both* beliefs as leading to salvation, — that is, as in some sense or other true, or at any rate not wholly false; altho it prefers the personal theory. "Arjuna said: 'Those devotees who thus with constant discipline revere Thee, and those who revere the Imperishable, the Unmanifest (i.e., the impersonal Brahman), which of these are the best knowers of discipline?' The Blessed One replied: 'Those who fix their minds upon Me and revere Me with constant discipline, pervaded with supreme faith, them I consider the best-disciplined. But those who revere the Imperishable, Indescribable, Unmanifest, Omnipresent, and Unthinkable, the Immovable, Unchangeable, Immutable, — restraining completely all their senses, and keeping their minds indifferent in all circumstances, devoted to the welfare of all creatures, — they too reach Me after all. Greater is the toil for those who fix their minds on the Unmanifest. For the unmanifest goal is hard for embodied creatures to attain.'"[27] Could we ask for any clearer proof of the thesis set forth in Chapter IV? The abstract, impersonal Absolute of the Upaniṣads was more than the mind of the average man could grasp. The Gītā represents a sort of compromise between that speculative

[24] x. 12.
[25] viii. 9.
[26] ix. 17, 18.
[27] xii. 1–5.

religion and popular theology. It provides an "easier way" to salvation, without denying the possibility of salvation to those hardier intellects which chose the more laborious, abstract path. We shall see later that in other ways, too, the Gītā tries to save men the trouble of mental exertion. It is quite characteristic of it to regard intellectual methods as difficult and unnecessary. It is "easier" for the ordinary man to worship a personal, anthropomorphic Deity than to fix his attention on an impersonal Absolute. So the Gītā, while allowing man to choose, recommends the belief in a personal God.

Elsewhere the impersonal Brahman is more or less distinctly subordinated to the personal God. Thus the following description is quite Upaniṣadic, except for the single phrase in which the Brahman is described as "ruled by Me": "The object of knowledge I will now set forth, knowing which one gains immortality; the beginningless Brahman, *ruled by Me*;[28] it is declared to be neither existent nor non-existent. It has hands and feet on all sides, eyes, heads, and faces on all sides, hearing on all sides, in the world; it permanently envelops everything. It has the semblance of the qualities of all the senses, but is free from all the senses; it is unattached, and yet it bears all; it is free from the strands, yet it experiences the strands (of material nature). Both without and within all beings; immovable and yet moving; because of its subtility it cannot be known; it is both afar off and near. Both undivided and as it were divided, it resides in (all) beings; it is to be known as the supporter of beings, and it is their consumer and their originator too. It, too, is called the light of lights, that is beyond darkness; knowledge, and the object of knowledge, and what is to be reached by knowledge; it is settled in the heart of all."[29] The impersonal Brahman is nominally granted all the dignity which the Upaniṣads claim for it — and yet it depends on the personal God. "For I am the foundation of Brahman!"[30] Other passages in which the Brahman is spoken of as the Supreme Soul, the One that is in all creatures, or the "Possessor-of-the-Field," leave us more or less uncertain as to just how the author would have formulated his thought if hard pressed. "When one perceives that the various estates of creatures are all fixed in One, and that it is just from that One that they spread out, then he attains Brahman. Because it is without beginning and free from the strands, this eternal supreme Soul (*ātman*), even tho it resides in the body, does not act, nor is it stained (affected, by actions). As the

[28] Literally, "having Me as the chief"; it is hard to determine the precise *nuance* of the phrase, but it seems to me to imply some subordination of the Brahman to "Me" (God). Others, by a different division of words, exclude the reference to "Me" from this passage. But xiv. 27, quoted below, is unambiguous and proves that my interpretation is at least possible.

[29] xiii. 12–17.

[30] xiv. 27.

omnipresent ether, because of its subtility, is not stained, so the Soul, residing in every body, is not stained. As the one sun illumines this whole world, so the Possessor-of-the-Field illumines the whole Field (material body)."[31] Is this impersonal, Upaniṣadic monism? Or is the One implicitly thought of under a personal, theistic guise? Or, as in the foregoing, is God the "foundation" of It? In a preceding verse[32] we were told that "I (God) am the Field-knower in all Fields"; this suggests that the "Possessor-of-the-Field" is regarded as the personal God. Again: "But higher than this (world of perishable beings) is another, eternal being . . . which perishes not when all beings perish. (This) unmanifest is called the eternal; they call it the highest goal, which having attained they do not return; *it is My supreme station* (or, *light*). This supreme spirit (*puruṣa*) is to be attained by single devotion; within it all beings rest; by it this universe is pervaded."[33] Again, we might think that we were reading a non-theistic Upaniṣad, but for the little phrase, "it is My supreme station (or, light)." Does this mean something else than that "Brahman is God"? Let the mystic answer. The fact seems to be that the author attempts to avoid careful definition of these terms. Or, to put it otherwise, he does not feel able to get rid of the Upaniṣadic Absolute, but he strives, perhaps unwittingly, to color it with his personal theism.

Elsewhere the theory of man as a dualism, a combination of "soul" and "body" or "material nature," leads to a macrocosmic dualism in which God, the Soul of the Universe, is set over against the cosmic or universal Prakṛti, "Material Nature" as a whole, which is then spoken of as *God's body,* as it were — God's material nature. So God too is dualistic; He has a double nature, a "lower" or material, and a "higher" or spiritual. "Earth, water, fire, wind, ether, thought-organ, consciousness, and I-faculty: thus is divided My material nature, eight-fold. This is (My) lower (nature). But know My other nature, higher than that. It is the Soul by which this world is sustained."[34] And just as the material nature of man confuses and deceives him, so that he thinks that what is really matter is himself (his soul), so he confuses God's body — manifest material nature — with God's unmanifest Self. "Deluded by these conditions of existence, composed of the Three Strands (*guṇas*, of material nature), this whole world fails to know Me, who am superior to them and eternal. For this is My divine illusion (*māyā*, trick, piece of jugglery), composed of the (three) strands, hard to get past. Those who resort solely to Me penetrate beyond this illusion."[35] "Foolish men conceive Me, the Unmanifest, as having become manifest. They do not know My higher nature, everlasting and supreme."[36]

[31] xiii. 30–33.
[32] xiii. 2.
[33] viii. 20–22.
[34] vii. 4, 5.
[35] vii. 13, 14.
[36] vii. 24.

The adherents of the Vedānta philosophy interpret such passages as meaning that material nature is "illusion" (*māyā*) in the sense that it does not really exist. I believe they are wrong. The Gītā only means that the Soul — universal Soul or God as well as individual soul — is utterly distinct from material nature or body; the "illusion" consists in the apparent blending of the two. The wise man should realize the distinction; but this does not imply the nonexistence of either. In my opinion the word *māyā* did not acquire its Vedāntic sense of "world-mirage" until long after the Gītā's time. The reality of material nature is clearly indicated in many passages in the Gītā. Thus it accepts the doctrine of evolution and devolution of all nature at the beginning and end of successive world-eons, a theory which is familiar in Hindu cosmogonic speculations, and makes God the "overseer" of the process, and *His* material nature the world-stuff out of which all material creatures evolve and into which they devolve. "All beings pass into My material nature at the end of an eon, and at the beginning of (the next) eon I send them forth again. Resting upon My own material nature, I send forth again and again this whole host of beings, which is powerless (by itself), by the power of (My) material nature. . . . With Me as overseer, material nature creates the world of moving and unmoving beings. This is the cause by which the world revolves."[37] This same process of successive creations in successive eons is alluded to elsewhere[38] and is there treated as wholly material, not even as supervised by the Supreme Soul, which however is mentioned in the following verses[39] as "higher than all that"; He does not perish when all beings perish at the end of an eon. But there is no suggestion in any of these passages that material nature is in any sense unreal.

In another very curious and interesting passage this creative activity is treated as a sexual relation between God, as the Supreme Soul (the male principle), and the female principle of inert or receptive matter. Instead of an evolution of beings out of matter independently of the Supreme Soul, or with Him merely as "overseer" of the process, the Supreme Soul or God "plants the germ" in the womb of nature, and from this union all beings evolve. But here — most curiously — the cosmic matter is not called by the usual name of Prakṛti, material nature, as we should expect[40] (altho this term would be peculiarly appropriate to such a connection, since the word *prakṛti* is grammatically of the feminine gender), but instead is called *Brahman*, which has neuter gender! "My womb is the great Brahman; in

[37] ix. 7, 8, 10.

[38] viii, 18, 19.

[39] viii. 20–22.

[40] And, be it noted, as later speculations call it; for this same sexual figure is used in later philosophy.

it I plant the germ. Thence comes the origin of all beings. Whatsoever forms originate in all wombs, of them great Brahman is the womb (mother); I am the father that furnishes the seed."[41] Brahman may be an equivalent for Prakṛti, material nature, in another passage also: "Whoso lays his actions upon Brahman and does his acts while avoiding attachment (or interest in the results; compare Chapter VII), to him evil does not cling, as water clings not to a lotus-leaf."[42] The context here permits, without compelling, the view that Brahman means "material nature," which is, as we have already seen, solely responsible for all actions. In these passages a strange fate has overtaken the Upaniṣadic Brahman. Originally the Soul of the universe, it has been so far degraded as to be definitely deprived of all spirituality, and identified with the inert cosmic Matter, which is precisely all that is *not* Soul. No more significant indication could be found of the Gītā's personal theism. For nothing could be clearer than the reason for this dethronement of the Brahman. It was impersonal; and so, logically, it must either make way for, or be absorbed by, the personal God of the Gītā. Of these two alternatives, the Gītā, with the catholicity of the true mystic, chooses both, and neither. As we have seen in this chapter, Brahman (1) is absorbed into God, who assumes all its characteristics; (2) is differentiated from God and placed in some sort of subordinate position to Him, or made a lower manifestation of Him; and (3) still at times retains its ancient prestige as the Absolute, the One-in-All. All these positions appear side by side in the Gītā. Often its references to the Brahman are so vague as to leave us in doubt as to just how the author was thinking of it for the moment.[43]

The whole material universe is, then, in some sense God's manifest form or material nature. But of far greater practical importance, for the development of the religion taught by the Gītā, is this further fact, that God, by the exercise of his *māyā* or "mysterious power," can and does take on empiric, personal existence as an individual being in the world of beings. "Tho I am unborn, tho My Self is eternal, tho I am the Lord of Beings, I resort to My own material nature and take on (empiric) being, by My own mysterious power."[44] This is of course a cardinal doctrine of the Gītā.

[41] xiv. 3, 4.

[42] v. 10.

[43] There is no clear indication that the Gītā knew the theory of the Trimūrti, the supreme triad consisting of Brahmā (as a masculine deity, the Creator-God), Viṣṇu, and Śiva, which is familiar in later Hinduism. Only once does the word Brahman in the Gītā have masculine gender unmistakably; in some of its occurrences the forms are ambiguous and could be either masculine or neuter, but when unambiguous it is always neuter except in a single instance. In that one occurrence (xi. 15) the god Brahmā is mentioned merely as one of the numerous beings that appear mystically manifested in the vision of the Deity's supreme form as revealed to Arjuna, in the eleventh chapter.

[44] iv. 6.

Kṛṣṇa, the principal speaker in the dialog, is himself such an incarnation of the Deity. He is not the only one; God appears upon earth again and again, to accomplish His purposes. And His purposes are expressed in the following famous verses: "For whenever right languishes, and unright shows its head, then I send Myself forth. To save the righteous, to destroy the wicked, to establish the right, I come into being in age after age." [45] God condescends to become man Himself, for the benefit of mankind. This is the beginning of the famous system of *avatārs* or incarnations of God, which became so characteristic of later Viṣṇuism and a prime source of its strength. No Christian community needs to be told how such a doctrine of a loving God who is born upon earth to save the world can conquer the hearts of men.

Of course, God appears in such an incarnation not in His true, supernal form. That form is not only invisible to the eye of man, or even of the (popular) "gods," but also unknowable to their minds. "I know all beings that have been, that are, and that shall be; but no one knows Me." [46] "The throngs of the gods know not My origin, nor the great seers (*ṛshis*); for I am the starting-point of the gods and the great seers altogether." [47] None but God Himself knows Himself, says Arjuna: "All this I hold to be true, that Thou tellest me; for neither gods nor demons know Thy manifestation, O Blessed One. Thou Thyself alone knowest Thyself by Thyself, O Supreme Spirit, Cause of being of Beings, Lord of Beings, God of Gods, Lord of the World." [48] But as a special act of grace, granted to the few whom God elects, and who serve Him with pure devotion, He may reveal His Supreme form. This He does to Arjuna, in the famous eleventh chapter of the Gītā, the climax of the poem — after first giving him a supernatural power of sight, since his natural eye could not behold the marvel.[49] The mystic vision is revealed by a pure act of God's grace. No amount of pious rites and performances can win it; it is granted only to the chosen of God, and, we are told, to Arjuna first of all mankind. "I in My grace have shown thee, Arjuna, this supreme form of Mine, by My own mysterious power; this majestic, universal, infinite, primeval form, which has not been seen before by any other than thee. Not by the Veda, by sacrifices or study, nor by almsgiving or rites or severe penance, can I be seen in this form by any other than thee in the world of men." [50] As to what Arjuna saw — of course, words fail utterly to describe it. It is the mystic's direct vision of God. The greater part of the eleventh chapter of the Gītā is devoted to the confessedly vain attempt to describe this indescribable. The ecstatic language of the description is hard to transfer to another tongue. Even in externals the passage differs from its surroundings; instead of the sober meter of most of

[45] iv. 7, 8.
[46] vii. 26.
[47] x. 2.
[48] x. 14, 15.
[49] xi. 8.
[50] xi. 47, 48.

the poem, it breaks forth into more elaborate lyric measures, which Sir Edwin Arnold imitates in his English version. The vision is described as "made up of all marvels." [51] "If the light of a thousand suns should suddenly burst forth in the sky, it were like His glory." [52] "Arjuna beheld the whole world there united, and yet infinitely divided, in the form of the God of Gods." [53] Therein were contained all creatures, the gods (Brahmā [54] and the rest), all the seers, the supernatural race of serpents, and all other beings; [55] there was neither beginning nor middle nor end to His form;[56] the sun and moon are His eyes, His face is flaming fire, He burns the whole world with His radiance.[57] And so on. We recognize the type of ecstasy which so many mystics of all times and lands have told of, and which, they all agree, can only be realized at first hand, not described in terms comprehensible to another unless the other be a brother-mystic who has himself enjoyed the experience.

[51] xi. 11.
[52] xi. 12.
[53] xi. 13.
[54] Here occurs the only unmistakable reference to the masculine God Brahmā that is found in the Gītā.
[55] xi. 15.
[56] xi. 16.
[57] xi. 19.

CHAPTER VII

ACTION AND REBIRTH

THE metaphysical views set forth in the last two chapters are to be understood as based upon or joined with the structure of general Hinduism which was briefly explained in my third chapter. It never occurred to the author of the Gītā to question the doctrines of pessimism, rebirth under the control of karma or "action," and salvation thru ultimate release from that round of rebirths. To him they are not so much points to be proved as underlying principles, which are axiomatic in quality. In emphasizing the immortality of the soul he compares the successive lives of an individual to successive states (childhood, maturity, old age) in one life, or to changes of garments: "As in this body childhood, young manhood, and old age come to the Embodied (Soul), so It proceeds to other bodies. The wise man is not confused in this." [1] "As, laying aside worn-out garments, a man takes on other, new ones, so laying aside worn-out bodies the Embodied (Soul) enters into other, new ones." [2] These existences are, of course, all bodily ones; and that means that they are subject to all the ills that afflict the body. For if, as we have seen, the Soul is in reality independent of the body, it is only the enlightened soul which succeeds in realizing this independence, in perceiving that what affects the body does not affect him. As long as, deluded by the material organ of self-consciousness, the "I-faculty," he imagines that *he* acts and suffers, so long he is enthralled, enchained in the round of existences. It is often stated, and always implied, that this chain is an evil, — that all bodily existence entails misery. Rebirth is called "the home (or source) of misery." [3] What results in its prolongation is therefore evil; what leads to release from it is or should be the chief aim of man. He who has obtained this release goes to the perfect state, *nirvāṇa*.[4]

When it comes to the details of the theory of rebirth and release from it, the Hindu systems are less unanimous, in spite of certain family resemblances. Common to all of them is the doctrine of "karma" or "action, deed," according to which, generally speaking, any action done must have its result, good or bad according to its moral quality, for the doer.[5] It fol-

[1] ii. 13.

[2] ii. 22.

[3] viii. 15.

[4] On which see above, page 125 f.

[5] We shall presently speak of the extent to which this principle is restricted in the teachings of the Gītā.

lows from this that in order to get rid of the chain of reincarnation, one must somehow or other be released or excused from the normally inevitable consequences of his actions — even good ones. Otherwise, *any* actions performed must have their fruit in continued existence.

The Gītā itself tells us that, as a consequence of such reasoning, "some wise men say that (all) action is to be abandoned as evil."[6] Such people choose the path of world-renouncing asceticism which has always had such an appeal to the men of India. In order to escape the effects of action, namely continued existence, they propose simply not to act — or to come as near to that ideal as possible. The ascetic life is advocated not only because it approximates a state of inaction and so tends directly to obliterate "karma," but also because withdrawal from the world is a kind of insurance against being entangled in worldly desires, which lead man astray from his true goal, emancipation. There are passages in the Gītā itself which recommend ascetic methods, such as carefully regulating the breath, fixing the eyes on a spot between the eyebrows, avoiding the "external contacts" of the senses with the objects of sense, holding in check the senses, the organ of thought, and the consciousness or will, and so devoting oneself solely to emancipation.[7] Even more explicitly and in greater detail another passage describes the ascetic practices of the "disciplined man." "The disciplined man should ever discipline himself, living alone in a secret place. . . . Arranging for himself in a clean place a steady seat that is neither too high nor too low, and that is covered with a cloth and a skin and *kuśa*-grass, there he should concentrate his mind, restraining the activities of his thoughts and his senses, and taking his place upon the seat should practise discipline unto self-purification. Holding his body, head, and neck even and motionless, he should steadfastly gaze at the tip of his nose and not look to one side or another. Abiding in the vow of chastity, his soul at peace and free from fear, restraining his mind, his thoughts fixed on Me (God), the disciplined man should sit absorbed in Me."[8]

These are not the only passages in which the Gītā uses expressions which suggest a more or less ascetic point of view. Yet such passages are decidedly rare in comparison with those which take the diametrically opposite position that one need not, indeed should not, renounce the world to live the life of a hermit, nor seek to refrain from actions. In general, the Gītā is opposed to asceticism or to renunciation of action as such. I suspect that this has been in large part responsible for its great influence. Altho the ascetic life has always appealed to more people in India, perhaps, than in any other land, still it has never been adopted in practice by more than a small minority. This is inevitable, in the nature of things. Asceticism is too

[6] xviii. 3. [7] v. 27, 28. [8] vi. 10–14.

violently opposed to natural human tendencies. The Gītā provides a religious justification for continuing an approximately normal human life. Therein lies its strength. It does not ask the impossible; and yet it furnishes religious inspiration. It holds out the hope of salvation on terms which are not out of the reach of the great mass of mankind. And it provides for its scheme of salvation a philosophic background, based on commonly accepted Hindu postulates.

As far as concerns the doctrine of "karma" or action as a cause of continued existence, the Gītā meets it in a very simple and convincing, and yet extremely clever, way. It reminds us that back of action lies *desire* or *passion* (either positive or negative, that is "love" or "hate"). It is passion that leads to actions, as we are told already in the Upaniṣads (see page 22), and still more emphatically in Buddhism and other classical Hindu systems. It is this that makes men interested in the results of actions. Now, the Gītā maintains that since desire or passion is more fundamental than action, it is desire, rather than action, which is man's enemy, and against which the preacher of religion must contend.[9] This not only seems very reasonable in itself, but it is quite in keeping with the general trend of higher Hindu religions.

But the Gītā is much more clear-cut and definite than most Hindu systems in deducing from this proposition the inference that there is no binding power in action *in itself*. If a man acts unselfishly, without interest in the result, the action has no effect on his fate; it leaves him free. "The wise call him intelligent all whose undertakings are free from desire and purpose, whose actions are consumed in the fire of knowledge. Abandoning attachment to the fruits of action, ever content, independent, he performs (in effect) no act whatsoever even when he sets out to act. Free from wishes, with controlled thoughts and soul, abandoning all possessions, and performing only acts of the body (not acting with the mind; that is, not feeling interest in his actions), he does not incur guilt. Content with getting what comes by chance, superior to the 'pairs' (of opposites, as pain and pleasure, heat and cold, and the like), free from jealousy, indifferent to success or failure, even when he acts he is not bound. Rid of attachment, free, his mind fixed in knowledge, acting only as a religious duty, all his acts are destroyed (that is, have no binding effect)." [10] Therefore one should act without interest in the result of the action, without "desire or hate." *Indifference* is the great desideratum. It is the same as inaction in effect. It guarantees freedom from the binding effect of "karma." "Whoso neither loathes nor desires is to be regarded as having permanently renounced (action). For he who is free from the 'pairs' (of opposites) is easily freed from the bondage (of existence)." [11] "He should not be delighted at attaining pleasure, nor

[9] iii. 34, 37. [10] iv 19–23. [11] v. 3.

should he be distressed at attaining pain." [12] He should "hold alike pleasure and pain, gain and loss, victory and defeat." [13]

As I have said, the Gītā goes so far as definitely to oppose the quietistic life. It advises participation in action, in the affairs of life, tho always with an unselfish spirit. "On action alone let thy interest be fixed, never on its fruits. Let not thy motive be the fruits of action; but cleave not to inaction." [14] "Therefore perform ever disinterestedly acts that should be performed. For in performing actions disinterestedly a man attains the highest." [15] "Whoso performs actions that should be performed, without interest in the fruits of action, he is the possessor of renunciation, he the disciplined man, and not he who (merely) abstains from (building the sacrificial) fires and from (ritual) acts." [16] It even goes so far as to hint at insincerity on the part of some renouncers of action, intimating that their thoughts may be more worldly than their actions; altho perhaps all that is intended is to emphasize in the strongest possible way the importance of the mental attitude, rather than of the physical act: "Whoso restrains his organs of action and sits pondering on the objects of sense with his mind, — his soul is deluded; he is called a hypocrite. But whoso restrains his sense-organs with his mind, and with his organs of action engages in discipline-of-action [17] (disciplined action), unattached (to the fruits of action), — he is superior." [18] Harsh penance or self-torture, as practised by some extreme sects of Hindu ascetics, is especially reprobated as doing violence to God, who is within man's person.[19] The true ascetic, according to the Gītā, is he who "renounces" not actions, but selfish interest in actions: "Renunciation of actions due to desires is what the sages hold to be (true) renunciation. Abandonment of the fruits of all actions the wise call (true) abandonment." [20] Moreover, the ascetic position is an impossible one, since *complete* cessation of action is out of the question; he who lives *must* act more or less.[21] God Himself acts, tho of course unselfishly; and of course He cannot be bound by action.[22] Without His action the world would not run; He keeps the universe going and thus sets an example of unselfish action to mankind, and the noble man should follow this example, thus himself setting an example for the common herd.[23] Action is inevitable because it is material nature

[12] v. 20.
[13] ii. 38.
[14] ii. 47.
[15] iii. 19.
[16] vi. 1. On the attitude of the Gītā towards established religion see my tenth chapter.
[17] We shall have more to say of "discipline" in Chapter VIII.
[18] iii. 6, 7.
[19] xvii. 6.
[20] xviii. 2.
[21] iii. 8; xviii. 11.
[22] iii. 20–25, especially 22; iv. 14; ix. 9.
[23] iii. 20 ff.

that acts, thru the power of past actions which compel future actions as their result; to seek to oppose the irresistible power of nature is folly.[24] "Not by not undertaking actions does a man attain to freedom from action, and not by mere withdrawal (ascetic renunciation) does he attain perfection. For there is no one whatsoever that remains even a single moment without performing actions. For every man is forced to perform actions willy-nilly, by the strands (the three *guṇas*) that spring from material nature."[25]

But granting that man should perform acts, and should not try to remain inactive, the question still remains, what kind of acts should he perform? Of course, whatever he does should be done in an unselfish spirit, without hope of reward or fear of suffering; but this is not a sufficiently explicit guide in choosing between the manifold possibilities of conduct that lie open to man. The Gītā tells us that "perfect action is called that which is *obligatory*, free from attachment, performed without desire or loathing, by one who does not seek the fruits thereof."[26] "Obligatory" here means, doubtless, required by religious duty; this is supported by some other passages: "Mankind is bound by action, with the exception of action whose object is *religious duty*;[27] perform action for that object, free from attachment (to its fruits)."[28] Religious, charitable, and penitential acts are not binding but "purifying," and should be performed.[29] In other passages, however, "duty" clearly includes acts which cannot possibly, by any stretch, be included in this category. Thus the "duty" of a kṣatriya, a member of the warrior caste, is to fight.[30] This is in keeping with a familiar traditional theory among the Hindus, according to which men have different natural duties according to the caste or station in life in which they are born. The performance of religious rites is the natural duty of brahmans; fighting (also giving of alms, protection of the people, and so forth) is that of warriors or nobles; commerce and husbandry of the vaiśya caste; service, of the śūdra caste, which theoretically consists of serfs. The Gītā accepts this theory, and even devotes several stanzas[31] to a definite statement of it, naive and primitive as it seems to us.[32] It says that a man should perform his own

[24] xviii. 60; iii. 33.

[25] iii. 4, 5.

[26] xviii. 23.

[27] The word here used means "worship," or more literally "sacrifice"; but it is used in the Gītā in a way which seems to include by extension any kind of duty enjoined by religion.

[28] iii. 9; cf. iv. 23, "if one acts for religious duty, all his acts are wiped out."

[29] xviii. 3, 5, 6.

[30] ii. 31.

[31] xviii. 41–44.

[32] As naive and primitive, let us say, as the theory that it is the natural duty of one man to work ten hours in a steel-mill, and that of another to spend five or six hours in a New York office managing the financial affairs of that mill and others.

native duty, that is, the duty which comes to him by birth, from the caste or station to which he belongs, "to which it has pleased God to call him," "even tho this duty be imperfect," rather than attempt a duty that pertains to another social group.[33] Again, with a different turn, man is told to do the things that are commanded of God, throwing the responsibility on Him, and not seeking to question His wisdom. By so doing, man is freed from the bondage of "karma."[34] It is sinful pride to refuse to obey God's commands, thinking that you know better than God.[35] We may see in these various discussions of "duty," as either innate in the social order or founded on divine commands, groping attempts to formulate definite answers to the very natural question, what concrete acts does "duty" require of man? But it is hardly possible to conceal the unsatisfactory nature of the Gītā's conclusions on this point. The writer, at least, cannot blame Arjuna for inquiring: "If thou holdest the attitude of mind to be more important than action, then why dost thou enjoin me to do this savage deed, O Kṛṣṇa?"[36] Why, indeed, should one fight and slay, even "unselfishly"? This eminently reasonable question is shamelessly dodged by Kṛṣṇa; no real answer is given — perhaps because none can be given.[37] And more often the Gītā attempts no concrete definition of duty, but contents itself with saying that man should do his duty simply because it *is* his duty, and with perfect indifference to the results — reminding us of Kant's categorical imperative.

We must, however, refer to another attempt to define duty which the Gītā repeatedly presents, and which not only furnishes a very high ethical standard, but is a logical deduction from the best Hindu metaphysics. If God is in all beings, if the soul or real self of all beings is One, it follows that "The wise look alike upon a learned and cultivated brahman, a (sacred) cow, an elephant, a dog, and an outcaste."[38] All beings are one in God;

[33] iii. 35; xviii. 45–48.

[34] iii. 30–32.

[35] xviii. 58, 59.

[36] iii. 1.

[37] I have tried to put the best possible light on the Gītā's teachings in this regard, and have ignored for this purpose certain verses in which the "duty" to fight is enjoined upon Arjuna on still lower grounds, as on the ground that he will be suspected of cowardice if he withdraws from the battle, and so will be despised of men (ii. 34 ff.; contrast xiv. 24, which says one must be indifferent to praise and blame), or even on the ground that if he is slain he will gain heaven (alluding to the popular Hindu belief in a sort of Valhalla for warriors slain in battle), while if he conquers he will enjoy rule over earth (ii. 37). These intrusions of popular ideas, while certainly unworthy of the philosophic standard of most of the Gītā, need not be considered interpolations. They simply illustrate the fact to which I have often alluded, that the Gītā is not a logical or systematic philosophical treatise, but a poem, containing many inconsistencies in ethical as well as metaphysical notions.

[38] v. 18. Dogs are very unclean animals in India.

by true knowledge "thou shalt see all beings without exception in thyself, and in Me."[39] "He whose soul is disciplined in discipline, seeing the same in all things, perceives himself in all beings, and all beings in himself,"[40] and "Me (God) in all and all in Me."[41] Accordingly one should behave in the same way towards friend and foe, kinsman and stranger, good men and bad;[42] namely, towards all as one would towards oneself. "Whoso looks upon all beings in the same way as upon himself, and sees likeness in all, whether it be pleasure or pain, he is deemed the supreme *yogin* (disciplined man)."[43] Those who are completely pervaded by the awareness of this truth, who feel that all beings are the same as themselves, that all as well as themselves are one with God, are freed from the effects of action and from rebirth; for they, of course, will not "injure themselves (in others) by themselves";[44] they "identify their own selves with the selves of all creatures, and even when they act are not affected ('stained') thereby."[45] "Even in this world, rebirth is overcome by those whose minds are fixed in indifference (the consciousness of sameness). For Brahman is flawless and alike (the same, in all creatures). Therefore such men are fixed in Brahman."[46] "Thou shalt love thy neighbor as thyself" — because thy neighbor *is* thyself; God is in both thee and thy neighbor, and both are in God. He who acts in this spirit need not fear that his acts will bind him to further existence.[47]

[39] iv. 35.
[40] vi. 29.
[41] vi. 30.
[42] vi. 9.
[43] vi. 32.
[44] xiii. 28.
[45] v. 7.
[46] v. 19.
[47] Compare Chapter XI.

CHAPTER VIII

The Way of Knowledge and the Way of Disciplined Activity

The dispute between those who held that all actions were binding, that is, involved man in continued existence, and those who maintained that acts performed with "indifference" to the results had no such effect, appears to have been only one aspect of a broader difference of opinion. So far we have spoken of what we have called the ascetic position as if it were a purely negative doctrine, teaching merely that man shall be saved by abstention from actions. But we learn from the Gītā that the school of thought against which its arguments on this subject are chiefly directed had a much more important positive theory of salvation, which is strictly in accord with the most fundamental principles of Hindu speculation from the Upaniṣads (and even before them) onward, and to which the Gītā itself feels forced to admit a considerable validity. This positive theory was no other than the "way of knowledge" which we met in Upaniṣadic thought, and which we traced back to its origins in the earliest Vedic speculations; the theory that by perfect knowledge man can control his destiny; that "the truth shall make" him "free."

So ingrained in Hindu culture is this belief in the power of supreme esoteric knowledge that probably no Hindu system would venture to deny it. The Gītā certainly does not. In many verses it recognizes it as explicitly as possible. "Even if thou shouldst be the worst of all sinners, merely by the boat of knowledge thou shalt cross over all (the 'sea' of) evil." [1] "As a kindled fire burns firewood to ashes, so the fire of knowledge burns all deeds to ashes," [2] that is, frees man from rebirth, the effect of deeds. Doubt, the opposite of knowledge, is fatal; the ignorant doubter cannot hope for bliss.[3] Man must "cut doubt with the sword of knowledge." [4] Knowledge is better than mere ritual religion: "Better than material sacrifice is the sacrifice (that consists) of knowledge. All action (karma) without remainder is completely ended in knowledge." [5] What knowledge? The knowledge of the supreme religious truth which each system professes to teach. Thus in the Gītā it is most often knowledge of God. Whosoever knows the mystic truth of God's nature is freed from rebirth and goes to God.[6] But elsewhere it is, for instance, the knowledge of the absolute separateness of soul and

[1] iv. 36.
[2] iv. 37.
[3] iv. 40.
[4] iv. 41, 42.
[5] iv. 33.
[6] iv. 9, 10; vii. 19; x. 3; xiv. 1 ff.

body, the independence of the soul from the body and all its acts and qualities, which brings release from rebirth.[7] In fact, the Gītā, like the Upaniṣads, tends to promise complete emancipation to one who "knows" any particularly profound religious or philosophic truth which it sets forth. This seems to have been characteristic of Hindu systems generally, at least in their early stages.

While different thinkers differed in their formulations of the supreme truth, by knowing which man should gain salvation, it appears that another and perhaps a more important difference, from the practical standpoint, was in their doctrines of method, or in the varying degrees of emphasis laid on various possible methods, for attaining enlightenment. The Gītā refers several times to such differences of method. In one passage it tells us that "some by *meditation* come to behold the Self (Soul, *ātman*) in the self by the self; others by the Sāṃkhya discipline, and others by the discipline of Action. But others, while not having this knowledge, hear it from others and devote themselves to it; even they too cross over death, by devoting themselves to what is revealed."[8] According to this, true knowledge — here spoken of as knowledge of the *ātman*, the Self or Soul (the context indicates that the author is thinking of the individual soul, as distinguished from matter, rather than of the universal soul) — may be gained in various ways: first, by inner meditation; then, by what is called the Sāṃkhya discipline, and by the "discipline of action"; and fourthly, by instruction from others, if one cannot attain to it by himself. All these methods are possible; all lead to salvation, to "crossing over death," which implies also escape from rebirth, since rebirth leads to redeath.

It is necessary to consider what the author means by the "Sāṃkhya discipline" and the "discipline of action." These are technical terms, which require very careful definition. The word which I translate "discipline" is *yoga*. The phrase "discipline of action" renders a Sanskrit compound, *karma-yoga*. Elsewhere the word *yoga* alone is used in the sense of *karma-yoga*; that is, "discipline," when otherwise undefined, means in the Gītā frequently (and indeed usually) the "discipline of action." The word *yoga* is unfortunately a very fluid one, used in a great variety of senses; this makes it often hard to give an exact definition of its meaning in any given occurrence. It may mean simply "method, means." It also means "exertion, diligence, zeal." And especially it is used to describe a regular, disciplined course of *action* leading to a definite end; in the Gītā and works of its type, to the end of emancipation. In some contemporary works it connotes a system of ascetic practices culminating in a sort of self-hypnosis, conceived as leading to emancipation, or to some supernatural attainment. When

[7] v. 16, 17 (cf. the preceding verses); xiv. 22–25.

[8] xiii. 24, 25.

used alone, without qualifying epithet, it always denotes, in works of the time of the Gītā, a *practical* method, as distinguished from an *intellectual* method. But in the Gītā its meaning is narrowed down. Here it means the method of salvation which is characterized by participation in normal, worldly action (hence the fuller expression *karma-yoga*, which is synonymous with *yoga* alone in this sense) without interest in the fruits of action. Action characterized by indifference is the central principle. "Yoga is defined as Indifference," says one verse.[9] But it is always an indifference *in action*. The word *yoga* definitely implies *activity*, as it is used in this connection in the Gītā, where it is constantly colored by (often unformulated) association with the other meaning of the word, "energetic performance, exertion." It is then opposed to the system or "rule" or "discipline" (the same word *yoga* is also used, confusingly) of the Sāṃkhya, which is elsewhere called the *jñāna-yoga* or "discipline of *knowledge*": "In this world a two-fold foundation (of religion) has been expounded by Me of old; by the discipline (or, method) of knowledge of the followers of Sāṃkhya, and by the discipline (or, method) of action of the followers of Yoga." [10]

The word *sāṃkhya* seems to mean "based on calculation"; that is, "philosophical, reflective, speculative method." [11] The adherents of this method believed in knowledge as the supreme and exclusive means of salvation, and in particular, according to the Gītā, they favored renunciation of all "works," of all activities. In the verses just following the one last quoted,[12] the Gītā's author argues against the policy of ascetic renunciation, clearly indicating that he is opposing the doctrine of the Sāṃkhya. In another passage *saṃnyāsa*, a regular term for ascetic renunciation, is contrasted with *karma-yoga*, "discipline of action," and in the next verse but one the same contrast is expressed by the terms *sāṃkhya* and *yoga*.[13] Further light as to the doctrines of the "Sāṃkhya" school is furnished by a passage in which a dissertation on the complete distinction between the soul and the body (see Chapter V) is followed by this verse: "This (preceding) is the point of view set forth in the Sāṃkhya; but hear now this (point of view set forth) in the Yoga." [14]

[9] ii. 48.

[10] iii. 3.

[11] Another theory is that it means "dealing with numbers," because the (later) system called by this name was characterized by many enumerated categories. Tho this interpretation is accepted by many distinguished scholars, it seems to me erroneous. See my article on "The meaning of *sāṃkhya* and *yoga*," *American Journal of Philology*, 45 (1924), 1 ff.; for the literal meaning of *sāṃkhya*, 35 ff.

[12] iii. 4 ff.

[13] v. 2, 4.

[14] ii. 39. The preceding passage referred to is the discussion summed up in ii. 30; there intervene a number of verses which are parenthetical and may possibly be a later interpolation, dealing with wholly unrelated matters. Practically all the rest of the Chapter (vss. 47–72) is devoted to explaining the doctrine of *yoga*, namely, indifference in action (cf. especially ii. 47, 48).

The "knowledge" which the Sāṃkhya taught, therefore, was or included the dualistic doctrine (familiarly accepted in the Gītā) that soul and body are two eternally separate entities.[15]

We have seen that many passages in the Gītā fully recognize the value of knowledge as a means of salvation. We have also found in various connections that the Gītā is very catholic and tolerant; that it is much inclined to admit validity to different points of view. We need not, therefore, be surprised to learn that in several places it definitely recognizes both the Sāṃkhya and the Yoga methods as effective. It even asserts that they are really one at bottom; which is simply another way of saying the same thing, that they both lead to salvation. "Fools say that Sāṃkhya and Yoga are different, not the wise. One who devotes himself only to one of these two obtains completely the fruit of both. The station that is obtained by the followers of Sāṃkhya is also reached by the followers of Yoga Whoso looks upon Sāṃkhya and Yoga as one has true vision."[16] "Renunciation (of action; that is, the 'way of knowledge' or the Sāṃkhya way) and discipline of action (*karma-yoga*; that is, the Yoga way) both lead to supreme weal."[17]

Yet the same verse of which I have just quoted a part goes on to say: "But of these two, discipline of action (*karma-yoga*) is better than renunciation of action (*karma-saṃnyāsa*)." And the reason, which is given a few verses later, is very interesting. "Renunciation, however, without discipline (*yoga*), is hard to attain. The sage who is disciplined in discipline quickly (easily) goes to Brahman."[18] Again, as above on page 48 f., we find the Gītā looking for the "easy way" to salvation, trying to meet the "man-in-the-street" half-way. It allows validity to the severe, more toilsome path of pure knowledge with ascetic renunciation of all activities. But few can travel that road. The Gītā appeals to the masses; that is why it has always

[15] I have felt it necessary to go into this matter somewhat technically because of the confusingly various ways in which these terms are used, and because of the further confusing fact that these same terms, Sāṃkhya and Yoga, are later applied to two systems of philosophy which have found many adherents in India but which I think did not exist in codified forms at the time of the Gītā. The later Sāṃkhya system is commonly said to be atheistic; and indeed some (by no means all!) of its adherents deny the existence of any World-soul or God. But there is no suggestion of such a view in the "Sāṃkhya" of the time of the Gītā (in my opinion; the contrary has been maintained, but I think wrongly). The later use of the term "Yoga" develops out of another sort of "practical activity" than that indicated by the Gītā as "Yoga." Professor Dasgupta in his *History of Indian Philosophy* (II. 455) rightly defines Sāṃkhya in the Gītā as "the path of knowledge," and (II. 476) sees that it does not mean "the traditional [later] Sāṃkhya philosophy." He comes fairly close to agreeing with my view of Sāṃkhya (apparently without knowing my article mentioned in note 11 above). I regret to say that I think he is utterly wrong on Yoga.

[16] v. 4, 5.

[17] v. 2.

[18] v. 6.

had so many followers. It claims that all the results which accrue to the follower of the strict intellectual method may also be obtained without withdrawing from action. Nay, it claims that even knowledge itself — the direct aim of the intellectual school — may be obtained thru disciplined activity: "For there is no purifier in the world like knowledge. He who is perfected in discipline (*yoga*) in due time finds it (knowledge) in himself." [19] From this point of view we may regard Yoga, disciplined activity, as an auxiliary means, useful in gaining the knowledge that shall bring release, just as devotion to God is elsewhere regarded in the same light.[20] This supports the thesis which I set forth in Chapter III,[21] that in Hindu speculation generally knowledge is to be regarded as the primary means of salvation, and all other methods are in origin secondary helps to the gaining of knowledge, however much they may come to overshadow the original aim.

In the Gītā, then, we find that the way of disciplined activity (*yoga*) is constantly favored at the expense of the way of knowledge and inactivity (*sāṃkhya*), despite the statements quoted above to the effect that either one is good enough as a means of salvation. Discipline and the practiser of discipline (the *yogin* or "possessor of *yoga*," or the *yukta*, "disciplined man") are constantly praised and exalted. "The disciplined man, renouncing the fruit of action, gains final blessedness. The undisciplined, because he acts wilfully (or, according to his lusts), being attached to the fruits (of action), is bound." [22] If one practises this sort of disciplined activity even imperfectly, that is, without completely realizing it in life, still the effect of it is not lost but continues in future births, bringing man ever nearer and nearer to full attainment, until at last, by perfection in discipline, salvation is gained.[23] Disciplined activity is superior not only to the "way of knowledge" but also to asceticism and to orthodox ritual religion: "The disciplined man (*yogin*, 'possessor of discipline') is superior to ascetics, and to the devotees of knowledge he is also considered superior, and to the devotees of (ritual) works he is superior; therefore be disciplined, O Arjuna." [24] It is significant, however, that "love of God" is *not* subordinated to disciplined activity in this list. On the contrary, the very next verse [25] adds that "the most perfectly disciplined man (*yuktatama*) is he who worships Me." In the next chapter we shall take up the method of devotion to God.

Readers may fairly ask for a more exact definition of what is meant by this "disciplined activity," this *yoga*. The Gītā does not fail to furnish it. It is implied by what has been said in this chapter and the preceding one. It consists in doing unselfishly whatever action seems to be required in any

[19] iv. 38.
[20] See page 173 f. below.
[21] Pages 127 ff.
[22] v. 12.
[23] vi. 37–45.
[24] vi. 46.
[25] vi. 47.

given circumstances; taking no interest in the results of the action to the doer, but not seeking to evade responsibility by refusing to act at all. The state of *yoga* is identified with "equanimity, stability of mind." It is described especially in a long passage in the second chapter of the Gītā, of which I quote selections here:[26] "Perform actions abiding in discipline, abandoning attachment (to the results), and being indifferent to success or failure; discipline is defined as indifference. For (mere) action is far inferior to discipline of mental attitude. Seek salvation in the mental attitude; wretched are those whose motive is the fruit (of action). He who is disciplined in mind leaves behind him in this life (the effects of) good and bad deeds alike. Therefore practise discipline; discipline in actions brings welfare. For the wise men that are disciplined in mind and abandon the fruits of action are freed from the bonds of rebirth and go to perfect bliss. . . . When one abandons all the desires of the mind and finds contentment by himself in his Self alone, then he is said to have 'stability of mind' (equanimity; synonym for 'discipline'). He whose mind is unperturbed by sorrow and without desire for pleasure, free from longing, fear, and wrath, is called a stable-minded holy man. He who has no desire towards anything, who getting this or that good or evil neither rejoices nor repines, his mind is stabilized. . . . For even the mind of an intelligent and earnestly striving man is violently carried away by the impetuous senses. Restraining them all he should abide in discipline, devoted to Me; for he whose senses are under control has a stabilized mind. . . . The man who abandons all desires and acts without longing, without self-interest and egotism, goes to peace."

In other passages special emphasis is laid on the meaning of the phrase "when one abandons all the desires of the mind and finds satisfaction by himself in his Self alone." What is meant is of course very different from what we mean by "selfishness." The idea is that internal joys are the only true ones; external joys, that is, those which result from the senses thru external stimulants, are both transitory and illusory. "With soul unattached to outside contacts, when he finds joy in the Self, his soul disciplined with the discipline of (i.e., that leads to) Brahman, he attains eternal bliss. For the enjoyments that spring from (outside) contacts are nothing but sources of misery; they are transitory (literally, 'they have beginning and end'); the wise man finds no pleasure in them. He who even in this life, before being freed from the body, can control the excitement that springs from desire and wrath, he is disciplined, he is blessed. Whoso finds his joy, his delight, and his illumination *within*, he, the disciplined, becomes Brahman, and goes to the *nirvāṇa* of (or, that is) Brahman."[27] "In which (state of *yoga*,

[26] ii. 48–72. The word "discipline" in my translation always renders *yoga*, and "disciplined" renders the corresponding participle *yukta*.

[27] v. 21–24.

discipline) the thought comes to rest, held in check by the practice of discipline, and in which, contemplating the Self by the Self, one finds satisfaction in the Self; in which he experiences that infinite bliss which is to be grasped (only) by the consciousness and is beyond the senses, and in which firmly established he cannot be moved from the truth; having gained which he realizes that there is no greater gain than it; established in which he is not moved by any sorrow, however great; he shall know this remover of all contacts with sorrow that is known as Yoga. This Yoga (discipline) should be practised with determination, with heart undismayed." [28] "But the man who finds his delight only in the Self, and his contentment and satisfaction only in the Self, for him there is (in effect) no action to be done. He can have no interest whatever in action done nor yet in action not done in this world, nor has he any dependence of interest in all beings (that is, he cannot be affected for either better or worse by anything from outside of himself)." [29]

Of particular interest is one verse which speaks of *moderation* in all things as a characteristic of the "disciplined" follower of *yoga*: "There is no discipline in him who eats too much, not yet in him who fasts completely; neither in him who indulges in too much sleep, nor yet in him who sleeps not at all." [30] This very pointedly emphasizes the opposition of the policy of "discipline" to that of asceticism, which was characterized by long-continued fasts, sometimes to the point of self-starvation, and by other extreme practices. This is one of the points of contact between the Gītā and Buddhism, for Buddhism too makes much of the doctrine of the "golden mean," opposing the extreme of self-torture as well as the extreme of worldliness.[31]

In closing this chapter I wish to reaffirm the fact that, in spite of occasional disparagements of the "way of knowledge," the Gītā's doctrine of disciplined activity really has an intellectual basis. The reason for acting with indifference is that actions cannot really affect the soul for good or ill; they concern matter exclusively. He who *knows* this will be steadfast in *yoga*, in indifference. This is brought out with admirable clarity in the last passage which I shall quote in describing the disciplined man: "As to both illumination and activity and delusion,[32] he neither loathes them when they appear nor longs for them when they have vanished (that is, he is indifferent to all

[28] vi. 20–23.

[29] iii. 17, 18.

[30] vi. 16.

[31] Similar expressions occur, to be sure, in late texts of the (later, systematic) "yoga" philosophy; and this point has been taken as an indication of interrelationship between the latter and Buddhism. See Oldenberg, *Upanishaden und Buddhismus*, 1st ed., p. 327; 2d ed., p. 282.

[32] These are the characteristic marks of the three "strands" of material nature, *sattva*, *rajas*, and *tamas*; see page 141.

material things). Taking part (in actions) as a disinterested participant, he is not perturbed by the (three) strands (of matter); he stands firm and unmoved in the thought that it is only the strands that are active. He is indifferent to pain and pleasure, and self-contained; clods of earth, stones, and gold are all one to him, pleasant and unpleasant things alike; he is wise (or, steadfast), and careless of praise or blame. Unmoved by honor or dishonor, alike to friend and foe, renouncing all enterprises, he is declared to have transcended the strands (of matter)."[33] In so far as the Gītā quarrels with what it calls the Sāṃkhya school, it is really not so much on the question of the power of knowledge, nor on the definition of what true knowledge is. It is rather because of the policy of complete abstention from actions which the Gītā attributes to the followers of Sāṃkhya. This is directly opposed to the doctrine of activity with indifference, which the Gītā usually preaches with all possible force — altho, as we saw in the last chapter, it contains passages which are inconsistent even with this.

[33] xiv. 22–25.

CHAPTER IX

The Way of Devotion to God

It has required something like a *tour de force* to reserve for this place a treatment of the relation of God to human salvation in the teachings of the Gītā. For in a sense it has involved temporarily ignoring the most cardinal doctrine of the poem. Yet the poem itself affords a precedent for approximately such an arrangement. The Gītā does not begin with this subject; and references to it in the early chapters are few and scattering. In the middle chapters of the work it gradually becomes more prominent, until it finally occupies the center of the stage, with the climax in the eleventh chapter, in which the mystic vision of God's supernal form is revealed to Arjuna.[1] After this, somewhat anti-climactically, the Gītā gradually drops into other themes again, to return to the theme of salvation thru God towards the end of its final, summary chapter (the eighteenth).

But in spite of our best efforts it has proved impossible to avoid some anticipation of this theme in the preceding chapters. In fact, with all the mixture of discordant theories which the Gītā contains, it is nevertheless so prevalently and devoutly theistic that its theism colors many of its expressions on other themes. So the various schemes of salvation, largely inherited from Upaniṣadic speculation, are reinterpreted in the Gītā in terms of its personal theism. The Upaniṣads taught that "knowledge" of the First Principle of the universe would lead to salvation. But the First Principle of the universe is God, declares the Gītā. It follows that knowledge of God is what brings salvation.[2] Freedom from rebirth comes from attainment — not of an impersonal First Principle, but — of God.[3]

Knowledge, however, whether of Brahman or of a personal God, is "hard to attain," as we have seen.[4] The difficulties of the intellectual method are emphasized in many places in the Gītā. Easier for the most of mankind is a more emotional scheme of salvation. This is what the Gītā furnishes by its famous doctrine of *bhakti*, "devotion" or "love of God." Tho not en-

[1] Page 155 f.

[2] Page 164.

[3] viii. 15, 16 etc.

[4] "Among thousands of men perhaps one strives for perfection. Even of those who strive and perfect themselves, rarely does one know Me in very truth." (vii. 3) "Hard to find is the noble soul who knows that Vāsudeva (a name for Kṛṣṇa = God) is all." (vii. 19) But: "Whoso always reveres Me with thoughts ever straying to no other object, for him I am easy to attain." (viii. 14)

tirely unknown to the Upaniṣads,[5] it is almost a new note in Hindu religious speculation. No doubt it originated in more popular forms of religion, which have left no written records. In the nature of things it could hardly be found, or at least could hardly be prominent, except in theistic religions. For "devotion" or "love" can hardly be felt except for a divine *personality*. That is why it is practically absent from the older forms of Hindu philosophic religion which are known to us.[6] Their divine principles were too impersonal. But we have good reason to believe that side by side with these abstract speculations there had long existed popular cults which worshiped various local gods and heroes; the Kṛṣṇa of the Bhagavad Gītā evidently originated as such a local deity. And it may fairly be taken for granted that in many or most of these cults devoted love of the god on the part of his worshipers, and perhaps vice versa, had played a considerable role.[7]

We have already seen that the Gītā's religion is a compromise between the speculation of the intellectuals and the emotionalism of popular religion. So the notion of *bhakti*, devotion, enters into its scheme of salvation by a side door, without at first displacing the old intellectual theory of salvation by knowledge. At least it is rationalized in this way. It is represented that by devoted love of God one can attain knowledge (of God), and so *indirectly* the salvation which comes thru this knowledge: "By devotion one comes to know Me, what My measure is and what I am in very truth; then, knowing Me in very truth, he straightway enters into Me." [8] So after the mystic revelation of his true form to Arjuna, Kṛṣṇa declares that such a revelation can come to a man thru no other means than devoted love: "But by unswerving devotion it is possible to know Me in this form, Arjuna, and to behold Me in very truth, and (so) to enter into Me." [9] Thus it is possible logically to reconcile the theory of devotion with the theory so often expressed that knowledge of God is what brings man to union with Him, that is, to salvation. Devotion to God is an auxiliary means of gaining knowledge of Him. It is significant that one of the Upaniṣad passages which men-

[5] See page 26 f.

[6] In the polytheism of the Rig Veda we do, indeed, find some traces of a relationship of love and trust between man and his gods, particularly as concerns the god Agni, the divine fire, who is found in every man's house and is "the friend of man." There is a wide gap, however, both in time and in spirit, between this and the "devotion" of the Bhagavad Gītā.

[7] The striking correspondence in externals between the Gītā's *bhakti* and the Christian love of God led some, in earlier days, to believe that the Gītā had borrowed the notion from Christianity. The correspondence is interesting, but it certainly does not justify such a theory. Undoubtedly, the two religions developed independently. The Gītā is now known to be almost certainly pre-Christian in date.

[8] xviii. 55.

[9] xi. 54.

tion the method of "devotion" speaks of it in the same way, as a means of getting knowledge.[10]

But not for long — if ever consistently — was the way of devotion subordinated to the way of knowledge. Usually the Gītā speaks of devotion as the immediate and all-sufficient way to final union with God. "Fix thy mind and devotion on Me; worship Me and revere Me. Thou shalt come even to Me by thus disciplining thy soul in full devotion to Me." [11] "Fix thy thought-organ on Me alone, let thy consciousness sink in Me, and thou shalt come to dwell even in Me hereafter; of that there is no doubt." [12] Even wicked men quickly become righteous and attain salvation thru devotion to God; even low-caste men, and women (who are a low grade of creatures), may be saved in the same way; "no devotee of God is lost." [13]

This quasi-miraculous salvation thru devotion is frequently represented as due to special divine intervention on behalf of the devotee. God, as it were, cancels the laws of nature for the benefit of his devoted worshipers, and brings them to salvation by divine grace. "But those who, laying all actions upon Me, intent on Me, meditate on Me and revere Me with utterly unswerving devotion, for them I speedily become the Savior from the ocean of the round of (rebirths and) deaths, because their thoughts are fixed on Me." [14] Therefore one should "abandon all (other) duties (or, religious practices or systems)" and make God his sole refuge; then "I will save thee from all evils; be not grieved!" [15] In another passage it is explained differently; God is represented as impartial to all men, having no favorites, but still the devotee is, by reason of his devotion, united with God: "I am alike to all beings; none is either hated or loved of Me. But those who revere Me with devotion — they are in Me and I too am in them." [16]

Even "discipline" (*yoga*), of which so much was said in the last chapter as a favorite way of salvation, is granted to the devotee by God. This again seems to suggest that devotion is not the immediate way to salvation, but a help towards it, in that it assists the devotee along the way — the way being here not the way of knowledge but that of "discipline." "To those ever-disciplined ones that revere Me lovingly, I grant the discipline of mind whereby they come unto Me." [17] In the very next verse God grants the light of *knowledge* to the devotee: "To show compassion to these same ones I, while remaining in My own true state, dispel their darkness that is born of ignorance by the shining light of knowledge." [18] All this simply amounts to saying that devotion is the way *par excellence* — that it is the key-road,

[10] See page 129.

[11] ix. 34.

[12] xii. 8; similarly viii. 7; xi. 55.

[13] ix. 30–32.

[14] xii. 6, 7.

[15] xviii. 66; cf. ix. 22.

[16] ix. 29.

[17] x. 10.

[18] x. 11.

which controls all other roads to salvation. The passage quoted at the end of the last chapter, describing the man who is perfectly disciplined and whose discipline is founded on true knowledge, is followed by this: "And he who serves Me with the unswerving discipline of *devotion*, transcends these strands (of matter) and is fit for becoming Brahman (that is, for emancipation)." [19] The way of knowledge and the way of disciplined activity are allowed their place; but the way of devotion controls them. Similarly after a passage [20] which sets forth the ascetic position, there is added the recommendation that the ascetic should fix his thoughts on God; by so doing he shall attain "the peace that culminates in *nirvāṇa*, and that rests in Me." [21] We referred above to the significant fact that in a passage glorifying "discipline" (*yoga*), the disciplined man is declared to be superior to ascetics, to followers of the path of knowledge, and to those who adhere to the rites of orthodox religion, but not to adherents of the method of devotion to God; on the contrary, "the most perfectly disciplined man is he who devoutly reveres Me, with his soul fixed on Me." [22] In one passage, which is curiously typical of the catholic or eclectic attitude which we have repeatedly noticed as characteristic of the Gītā, we are given to understand that God may be reached (and this implies complete emancipation) in several ways. First, we are commanded to sink our hearts completely in loving devotion to God. "However, if thou canst not fix thy thoughts steadfastly on Me, then seek to win Me by discipline of practice (that is, by what is elsewhere called simply *yoga*, 'disciplined activity'). If incapable even of practice, be wholly devoted to work for Me; by performing actions for My sake (as described in the next paragraph) thou shalt also win perfection. But if thou art unable even to do this, resorting to My discipline then make abandonment of all fruits of action (that is, act unselfishly, as set forth in Chapter VII), controlling thyself." [23] The way of devotion is the favorite one to the author of the Gītā; but he admits the validity of other ways too, if for personal reasons a man finds them preferable. Still oftener, all these various ways are more or less vaguely blended and felt as in the last analysis essentially one; but the devotional coloring is perhaps the most constant characteristic of the blend.

As indicated in the last quotation, the attitude of devotion to God has an important bearing on the question of action and its results under the doctrine of karma, discussed in my seventh chapter. Not only does duty require that one should do the commands of God,[24] but a sure way to escape any of the normal results of action, in continued rebirth, is to "do all as a gift to God" or to "resign all actions to God"; that is, to throw upon Him

[19] xiv. 26.
[20] Quoted above, page 158 f.
[21] vi. 15.
[22] vi. 47; see page 168.
[23] xii. 9–11.
[24] iii. 30–32.

all responsibility for actions; if one acts only in a spirit of loving devotion to God and of trust in Him, relying upon Him to settle the matter, He will save the devotee from the effects of action; that is, from further rebirth. "Whatever thou doest, whatever thou eatest, whatever thou offerest (in oblation), whatever thou givest, whatever austerity thou performest, that do as a gift to Me. Thus thou shalt be freed from the bonds of action with its fruits, whether good or evil; thy soul shall be disciplined in the discipline of renunciation, and thou shalt be freed and shalt attain unto Me." [25] Let a man perform his own natural duty [26] as a service to God: "A man finds perfection in worshiping Him from whom comes the activity (or, origin) of all beings, by whom this universe is pervaded — *by doing action appropriate to himself*." [27] "Taking refuge in Me, tho ever performing all acts, by My grace a man attains the eternal, undying station. Casting mentally all acts upon Me, devoted to Me, cleaving to discipline of mind, keep thy thoughts ever fixed on Me." [28] "Thinking on Me, by My grace thou shalt cross over all difficulties"; refusal to do so would be a sign of pride and self-conceit, an indication that man thinks he knows more than God; such a man would perish; and he could not, after all, avoid the acts to which his nature impels him; "material nature will coerce" him.[29] Nor need man fear that anything done in true, loving devotion to God will be ignored by Him. God accepts the humblest offering of His devotees, taking it in the spirit in which it is meant: "If a man offers Me with devotion (*bhakti*) a leaf, a flower, a fruit, or a sip of water — that loving gift of My devotee I accept (literally, I eat)." [30]

It is specially important that one should fix his mind on God at the time of death. According to a familiar belief among the Hindus, the attitude of mind at the hour of death is particularly influential in determining man's state after death.[31] The following verse of the Gītā expresses the traditionally accepted view: "Whatever condition of being one meditates on as he leaves the body at death, precisely to that condition he goes, his whole nature being infused therewith." [32] That is why to this day all pious Hindus

[25] ix. 27–28.
[26] Cf. page 161.
[27] xviii. 46.
[28] xviii. 56, 57.
[29] xviii. 58, 59.
[30] ix. 26.
[31] Indeed, according to the Gītā (viii. 23–27), the time of death is so important in determining man's future fate, that the "disciplined man" and "knower of Brahman" attains freedom from rebirth if he dies at a favorable time, but is reborn again if he dies at an unfavorable time. Favorable times are "fire, light, day, the bright half of the lunar month (when the moon is waxing), the six months during which the sun moves northward." Their opposites are unfavorable. There are interesting parallels in Christian and Jewish ideas on the importance of the "hour of death"; see Edgerton, "The Hour of Death," *Annals of the Bhandarkar Institute* (Poona), 8. 219 ff.
[32] viii. 6.

meditate on their respective sectarian deities, and recite their sacred mantras or holy formulas, at the hour of death, hoping thereby to gain salvation. Accordingly the Gītā does not hesitate to promise this result to one who meditates on God at death: "He who at the hour of his death passes out and leaves his body while meditating on Me alone, goes to My estate; of this there is no doubt."[33] "(Whosoever thinks on God) at the time of his death with unswerving mind, disciplined (*yukta*) in devotion (*bhakti*) and in the power of discipline (*yoga*) too, making his breath to pass wholly into the space between his eyebrows, he goes to that supreme, divine Spirit (*puruṣa*). . . . Pronouncing the single (sacred) syllable Om (which is) Brahman, thinking upon Me, he who (thus) leaves the body and dies goes to the highest goal."[34]

The characteristics of the perfect devotee of God are very much like those attributed to the possessor of "discipline" as described in the last chapter. Indeed, the two are really one. The true possessor of "discipline" will be devoted to God; devotion to God involves or brings with it perfection in discipline. Perhaps the note of joy, of bliss, is more definitely present in descriptions of the devotee than of the "disciplined" man. "Those whose thoughts and lives are centered upon Me, who are ever enlightening one another and telling about Me (giving 'testimony,' as some Christian sects say), are filled with joy and contentment."[35] The true devotee is described in the following passage: "Not hostile to all creatures, friendly and compassionate, unselfish and without egotism, indifferent to pain and pleasure, patient, contented, ever disciplined, self controlled, of firm resolve; he who is devoted to Me and has fixed his mind and consciousness upon Me, is dear to Me. Before whom people do not tremble and who does not tremble before people, who is free from the excitement of joy, impatience, fear, and agitation, he too is dear to Me. Unconcerned, pure, capable, disinterested, imperturbable, abandoning all undertakings, — such a devotee of Mine is dear to Me. Who neither delights nor loathes, neither grieves nor craves, who renounces pleasant and unpleasant objects, and is full of devotion, he is dear to Me. Who is the same to friend and foe, indifferent to honor and disgrace, to heat and cold, to joy amd sorrow, who has abandoned all attachment, to whom praise and blame are all one, restrained in speech, content with whatsoever (his lot may be), having no fixed habitation, of steadfast mind, full of devotion, he is dear to Me. But those devotees of Mine who believe and accept this nectar of religious doctrine as I have expressed it (in the Bhagavad Gītā), intent on Me, they are beyond measure dear to Me."[36]

[33] viii. 5.

[34] viii. 10, 13.

[35] x. 9.

[36] xii. 13–20.

The very heart, the quintessence, of the doctrines of the Gītā is declared by Hindu commentators to be found in this verse:[37] "He who does My work, who is devoted to Me and loves Me, who is free from attachment (to worldly things) and from enmity to all beings, goes to Me, Son of Pāṇḍu!"

[37] xi. 55.

CHAPTER X

Attitude Towards Hindu Orthodoxy and Other Religious Beliefs

The curious many-sidedness, tolerance, or inconsistency — whichever one may choose to call it — of the Bhagavad Gītā, which we have noted in nearly every chapter of this book, is shown nowhere more strikingly than in its attitude towards what we may call orthodox, established religion.

By this I mean the system of traditional sacrifices and observances, founded ultimately upon the Vedic cult, which became accepted by Brahmanism and were in the time of the Gītā, and have remained even to this day, theoretically incumbent upon all pious Hindus, at least of the upper castes. This system of rites implied and implies very little in the way of beliefs. It was and is, almost exclusively, a matter of formal observances. It is a matter of conformance to traditional propriety in actions; so long as one conforms outwardly, it makes little difference what he believes inwardly. It does, to be sure, imply recognition of the privileged status of the brahman caste, as the hereditary custodians of the cult, and the nominal leaders of society. No sacrifice was supposed to be valid unless a brahman was hired to perform it.

The original theory of this orthodox cult is fairly stated in the Bhagavad Gītā: "The gods, being prospered by sacrifices, shall grant you the enjoyments you desire. He who without giving to them enjoys their gifts is nothing but a thief."[1] That is, it is a matter of commerical bargaining between the old, traditional gods (not to be confused with the God of the Bhagavad Gītā!) and men. The gods control benefits, and grant them in exchange for the gratifications of the sacrifice. It is man's duty to furnish these gratifications; otherwise he would be getting something for nothing. In this passage the Gītā unhesitatingly commends this system. It even says that actions of the sacrifice have no binding effect,[2] and that sacrificers "are freed from all sins,"[3] altho, to be sure, it adds that it is wicked to perform even such acts "selfishly,"[4] — a statement that is hardly consistent with the theory of the ritual cult just quoted, which seems to imply that the whole basis of it is a matter of selfish interest. The fact is, however, that this theory, which is inherited from Vedic times, is not ordinarily brought out clearly in the Gītā or in other later religious texts. It is more often ignored or slurred over. The Gītā contains passages in which sacrificial

[1] iii. 12.
[2] iii. 9.
[3] iii. 13.
[4] iii. 13.

acts are spoken of as part of man's duty and to be performed simply *qua* duty — "abandoning attachment."[5] "Actions of sacrifice, alms, and penance are not to be abandoned; on the contrary they are to be performed. Sacrifice, alms, and penance are purifying for the wise. But even these actions are to be performed with abandonment of attachment and (of desire for) their fruits; that is my definite and final judgment."[6] "Sacrifice which is offered as contemplated by injunctions, by men who are not seeking the fruits thereof, simply because it is their duty to sacrifice, concentrating their minds, that is sacrifice of the highest quality."[7]

Otherwise it is possible by a mystic or symbolic interpretation of the word "sacrifice" to make it mean, or include, things which are quite different from commonplace ritual performance, and more in keeping with the general trend of the Gītā's teachings. In one passage we find indeed a statement which sounds like a thoro-going acceptance of the ritual dogma: "Those who eat the nectar of the leavings of the sacrifice go to the eternal Brahman. Not even this world, still less any other, is for him who does not sacrifice."[8] But in the surrounding stanzas[9] the word "sacrifice" is interpreted as including many different kinds of religious practices: restraint of the senses, devotion to the Brahman, ascetic austerities, "disciplined activity" (*yoga*), study, and "knowledge"; and all these are recognized[10] as forms of "sacrifice" that have their validity. It is added that "the sacrifice of knowledge is better than material sacrifice; all action (karma) without remainder is completely ended in knowledge."[11] The "sacrifice of knowledge" means, of course, the intellectual method of salvation, and equally of course it has nothing whatever to do with ritual sacrifices. It is only by mystic symbolism that the term "sacrifice" can be applied to it at all.

On the other hand there are not wanting in the Gītā passages which definitely disparage the ritual religion. "Those who take delight in the words of the Veda" are called "undiscerning," "full of desires, aiming at heaven"; their doctrines "yield rebirth as the fruit of actions," and are "replete with various rites aiming at the goal of enjoyment and power."[12] "The Vedas belong to the realm of the three strands (of material nature); be thou free from the three strands!"[13] The really wise man has no more need for the "knowledge" of the Vedas (the word Veda means "knowledge") than he needs a water-tank (for irrigation) when there is a general flood.[14] If so pronounced a polemic attitude is exceptional, there are various other passages which treat the ritual religion with scant respect. A man who gets

[5] iv. 23.
[6] xviii. 5, 6.
[7] xvii. 11.
[8] iv. 31.
[9] iv. 23–33.
[10] iv. 30.
[11] iv. 33.
[12] ii. 42, 43.
[13] ii. 45.
[14] ii. 46.

out of the "jungle of delusion" will become disgusted with the revealed religion or holy "tradition," and in turning against this holy "tradition" he will acquire discipline (*yoga*).[15] God's true form can never be known thru religious works.[16] He does not reveal Himself to the adherents of the traditional cult, not even to the gods to whom that cult is devoted, who long in vain for a sight of Him;[17] they know nothing of His nature and origin, and the seers (*ṛshis*) who are the reputed authors of the Vedic hymns are equally ignorant.[18]

The orthodox cult is put in its place, so to speak, in the statement that "those who desire the success of (ritual) acts sacrifice in this world to the gods."[19] That is, if you want the sort of thing that sacrifice is designed to accomplish, by all means sacrifice, and you will get it. It is a low sort of aim; but such as it is, if one honestly seeks it, he shall find it. And that precisely because of his sincerity and devotion to what he conceives, however mistakenly, to be his religious duty. "Those who are deprived of knowledge by this or that desire (for some fruit of religious actions) resort to other deities (than Me); they take up various religious systems, being constrained by their own natures."[20] If they are sincere, they get the fruit they seek; but it is the one true God, whom they know not, who gives it to them. "Whoever seeks to worship with true faith and devotion any (other) form (of deity), for him I make that same faith unswerving, and, being disciplined in that faith, he devotes himself to worship of that (form of deity), and obtains therefrom his desires, since it is none but I that grant them!"[21] True and righteous ritualists, "worshiping Me by means of sacrifices," duly succeed in gaining the sensuous heaven which is one of the traditional rewards of ritualism, and enjoy divine pleasures there.[22] But of course this is a very limited form of success. Such "heavenly" existences are finite; they belong to the round of rebirths just as much as do earthly human lives. When the effect of their religious merit is exhausted, such men fall to earth again.[23] All that has nothing to do with the real goal of man, which is release from *all* existence.

What is true of orthodox ritualism is true of all other sorts of religion. Any religion is better than none. Whole-hearted and unqualified condemnation is reserved for those "demoniac" (wicked) men who "say that the world is untrue, without any basis (religious principle upon which to rest), without God, not produced by regular mutual causation, in short, motivated by desire."[24] The "materialistic" school here referred to is accused by its

[15] ii. 52, 53.
[16] xi. 48.
[17] xi. 52, 53.
[18] x. 2, 14.
[19] iv. 12.
[20] vii. 20.
[21] vii. 21, 22.
[22] ix. 20.
[23] ix. 21.
[24] xvi. 8.

opponents of having taught that all religion and philosophy were nonsense; that there was no guiding principle in the world; that all was chance; that the alleged moral law of the effect of deeds on the doer was baseless; that there was no soul, and no life after death; and that consequently the wise man was he who devoted himself to getting as much worldly enjoyment out of life as he could. Such doctrines are of course abhorrent to the Gītā, as to all the accepted forms of Hinduism. On the other hand, those who genuinely tho erroneously worship other gods are really worshiping the true God, tho they do not know it; and God accepts their worship, imperfect tho it be. "Even those who are devoted to other deities and worship them, filled with faith, they too really worship Me, tho not in correct fashion. For I am both the recipient and the lord of all worship (literally, 'of all sacrifices'). But they do not know Me aright. Therefore they fall."[25] "They fall"; that is, the "heavenly" rewards which they attain are finite, and upon the exhaustion of the merit acquired by their sincere tho mistaken religious practices, they return to ordinary worldly life again. "But finite are these fruits which come to such ignorant men. Those who revere the (popular or ritualistic) gods go to the gods; those who revere Me go to Me."[26] So each religion brings its suitable reward. "Votaries of the gods go to the gods; votaries of the 'fathers' (spirits of the dead), to the 'fathers'; worshipers of the goblins go to the goblins; My worshipers also go to Me."[27] And, as the last paragraph shows, it is really thru the one God that the followers of other religions gain their objects. Since those objects are necessarily imperfect and limited, because their seekers are by definition ignorant of the true goal of man, it remains true that one should "abandon all (other) religious duties" and make (the one true) God alone his refuge.[28]

[25] ix. 23, 24.
[26] vii. 23.
[27] ix. 25.
[28] xviii. 66.

CHAPTER XI

Practical Morality

The Gītā's attitude toward practical morality is characteristic of most Hindu religions. In its relation to the ultimate goal of salvation, morality is only a secondary means. It alone is never sufficient to achieve that goal. But on the other hand it leads to ever better and higher existences, and helps to prepare for final success.

The importance of morality comes out most clearly on the negative side. Immorality is clearly regarded as a serious, indeed usually a fatal, hindrance.[1] To be sure we are told that "if even a very wicked man worships Me with single devotion, he is to be regarded as righteous after all; for he has the right resolution";[2] and again that "even if thou shouldst be the worst sinner of all sinners, thou shalt cross over all (the 'sea' of) evil merely by the boat of knowledge."[3] These passages suggest a sort of magic absolution from sin by devotion to God, or to knowledge, as the case may be. It might be inferred from them that it makes little or no difference what a man may do, so long as he succeeds in possessing himself of the key to salvation. This is, however, probably not a fair inference from the Gītā's words. In the first place we must remember that the Gītā is poetic in its language and not infrequently emphasizes its ideas by a certain overstatement. To drive home the importance of "devotion" or "knowledge" it attributes to each of them in turn the power to absolve from the most heinous sins. Secondly, the Gītā undoubtedly means to imply a reformation and repentance on the part of the sinner as a prerequisite, or at least concomitant, to the attainment of "devotion" or "knowledge." We are, indeed, told elsewhere in definite terms that wicked men cannot, in the nature of things, possess true devotion or knowledge either. "Wicked and deluded evil-doers do not resort to Me; their intelligence is taken away by (My) illusion (*māyā*), and they remain in the 'demoniac' condition."[4] (We shall see what is meant by the "demoniac" condition in the next paragraph.) In another passage "knowledge" is defined at length in distinctly ethical terms; that is, he who is wise is necessarily also righteous, as Socrates said. Knowledge includes "absence of pride and deceit, harmlessness, patience, uprightness, devotion to one's teacher,

[1] xvi. 22, which means to imply only that one must get rid of immorality first, before seeking the way to salvation.

[2] ix. 30.

[3] iv. 36.

[4] vii. 15.

purity, firmness, self-control, aversion to the objects of sense, unselfishness," and so forth; "indifference" and "devotion to God" are also included.[5] Again a description of the qualities of the perfected man, who is fit for union with Brahman, includes abstention from lust and hatred and from such vices as selfishness, violence, pride, desire, and anger.[6]

The sixteenth chapter of the Gītā is wholly devoted to a sort of practical moral code. It tells us that there are two kinds of "nature" or "condition" or "estate" of man, the "divine" and the "demoniac"; that is, the good and the bad, the sheep and the goats. The good estate tends towards emancipation, the bad towards continued bondage in existence.[7] That is, more explicitly, men who are bad or "demoniac" by nature are reborn again and again; they fail to reach God, and their fate is wretched,[8] while the good come finally to salvation.[9] The good are characterized by "fearlessness, purification of being, steadfastness in the discipline of knowledge (or, knowledge and disciplined activity), generosity, self-control, sacrifice, (religious) study, austerities, and uprightness; harmlessness, truth, freedom from anger, abandonment (or, generosity), serenity, freedom from malice, compassion to all creatures, uncovetousness, gentleness, modesty, no fickleness; majesty, patience, fortitude, purity, non-violence, freedom from pride."[10] The characteristics of the wicked are described and illustrated at much greater length. In general they are, of course, the opposites of the qualities just mentioned. But emphasis is laid on the ignorance of the wicked,[11] on their materialistic and atheistic philosophy,[12] on their overweening pride and stupid self-confidence.[13] "Resorting to egotism, violence, arrogance, lust, and wrath, they hate Me in their own bodies and those of others, these envious men";[14] that is, by their misdeeds they wrong God, who is in themselves and in other men. All their vices are finally traced to three primary vices, desire or lust, wrath, and greed, "a threefold gate to hell, destroying the soul."[15] He who is subject to them cannot hope for perfection or bliss.[16] In another passage desire or lust and wrath are referred to as the twin causes of all vice.[17] This seems indeed sufficient, since avarice or greed is only a specialized form of desire or lust. "Desire and loathing" is the formula in other places.[18] And since "loathing" is merely negative desire, while "wrath" or "passion" is only a pragmatic manifestation or result of desire, whether positive or negative, we find that in the last analysis "desire" is the root of all evil.[19]

[5] xiii. 7–11.
[6] xviii. 51–53.
[7] xvi. 5.
[8] xvi. 20.
[9] xvi. 22.
[10] xvi. 1–3.
[11] xvi. 7.
[12] xvi. 8; cf. page 79 f.
[13] xvi. 13 ff.
[14] xvi. 18.
[15] xvi. 21.
[16] xvi. 23.
[17] iii. 37.
[18] E.g., iii. 34.
[19] Cf. pages 124 and 160 above.

One positive feature of the Gītā's morality deserves special mention. As we saw above at the end of Chapter VII, the metaphysical doctrine that the one universal Soul is in all creatures furnishes an admirable basis for a very lofty type of morality. Since one's own Self or Soul is really identical with the Self or Soul of all other creatures,[20] therefore one who injures others injures himself. "For beholding the same Lord (the universal Soul) residing in all beings, a man does not harm himself (his own self in others) by himself; so he goes to the final goal." [21] Thus one of the most striking and emphatic of the ethical doctrines of the Gītā is substantially that of the Golden Rule. Man must treat all creatures alike, from the highest to the lowest,[22] namely like himself.[23] The perfected man "delights in the welfare of all beings." [24] This principle is usually regarded as perhaps the highest formulation of practical ethics that any religion has attained. It is interesting to see how naturally and simply it follows from one of the most fundamental tenets of the Gītā's philosophy.

A genuine application of this moral principle would seem almost inevitably to include avoidance of any violent injury to living beings. And, as is well known, most Hindu sects have in fact applied it in this way, at least in theory, and to a considerable extent in practice. "Non-violence" or "harmlessness" (*ahiṃsā*) has generally been accepted as a cardinal virtue. It finds expression for instance in the vegetarian diet which so many Hindus have always favored, and in the policy of pacifism and "passive resistance" which, while never adopted universally, has probably had more followers at every period in India than in most other lands.

The Gītā's morality on this point is somewhat disappointing. It does indeed include "harmlessness" or "non-violence" (*ahiṃsā*) in several of its lists of virtues.[25] But it never singles it out for special emphasis. It seems to be content to let it lie buried in such more or less formal moral catalogs. One gets the impression that it was too prominent and well-recognized a virtue to be ignored; so some lip-homage is paid to it. But it is never definitely and sharply applied in such a form as "Thou shalt not kill." The Gītā contrasts strikingly in this respect with some other Hindu sects, such as the Buddhists and (still more) the Jains. It seems a little strange, at first sight, to find any Hindu religious text treating the doctrine of non-violence in so stepmotherly a fashion. But of course the reason is quite evident. The Gītā is hampered by the fact that it is supposed to justify Arjuna's partici-

[20] iv. 35; v. 7; vi. 29, etc.

[21] xiii. 28.

[22] v. 18; cf. vi. 9.

[23] vi. 32.

[24] v. 25.

[25] xiii. 7 and xvi. 2, quoted on pp. 183, 184; also x. 5 anl xvii. 14.

pation in war. This dramatic situation is alluded to repeatedly, and the author seems to have it in the back of his head a large part of the time. To be sure, many of his doctrines are inconsistent enough with such a purpose, as we have abundantly seen. And we must not forget, either, that "non-injury" is clearly implied in the Gītā's teachings on the subject of unselfishness and doing good to others. That is, to carry out these teachings in any real sense would necessarily involve doing no harm to living creatures. But to lay a frank and full emphasis upon this principle, to follow it out explicitly to its logical conclusion, would mean to run so glaringly counter to the professed aim of the piece, that it is not strange that the author avoids doing so. Even his catholicity seems to have shrunk from such an inconsistency as that. We can hardly help feeling, however, that he lost a golden opportunity thereby.

INTERPRETATION OF THE BHAGAVAD GĪTĀ

THIRD PART

SUMMARY AND CONCLUSION

CHAPTER XII

Summary

FIRST PART: PRELIMINARY CHAPTERS

Chapter I. *Introductory.* — The Bhagavad Gītā, the Bible of Kṛṣṇaism, is dramatically a part of the Mahābhārata. Its ostensible purpose is to prove to Arjuna, one of the heroes of that epic, the necessity and propriety of taking part in the battle which is the epic's main theme. In actual fact, it is a mystic poem, dealing with the nature of the soul and body of man, man's relation to God, and the way or ways by which man is to attain salvation. It is poetic, mystical, and devotional, rather than logical and philosophical. It contains many discordant doctrines; to try to unite them all in a consistent system is to do violence to its spirit. In this respect it is like all Hindu speculative literature of its time and earlier, — particularly like the Upaniṣads, to which it is deeply indebted. Like them, too, it is practical in its attitude, seeking religious or philosophic truth not for its own sake but as a means of human salvation.

Chapter II. *The Origins of Hindu Speculation.* — Out of the ritualistic polytheism, based on nature-worship, of the Rig Veda, developed on the one hand the pure ritualism of the Brāhmaṇa texts, on the other hand tentative speculations leading towards either monotheism or monism, — seeking to explain the constitution of the universe and of man in terms of a unitary principle. This unitary principle is at first often described concretely and physically; but with the passage of time the tendency is towards ever more abstract and metaphysical terms, culminating in such expressions as "the Existent" (*sat*), or "the Self, Soul" (*ātman*). The influence of ritualistic terms is also evident, particularly in the use of the Brahman, the embodiment of the ritual religion, as a name for the principle of the universe. From very early times the texts set up a parallelism between the universe, the macrocosm, and man, the microcosm.

Chapter III. *The Upaniṣads, and the Fundamental Doctrines of Later Hindu Thought.* — In the Upaniṣads this parallelism becomes an identity, by the Brāhmaṇa principle of mystic identification: the Soul of the universe is identified with the Soul of man, and by this identification man hopes to "know" and so magically to control the universe, which is declared to be his self. In the Upaniṣads, too, we find the first clear statements of the basic axioms of later Hinduism, which may be summed up as follows. First, *pessimism*: all empiric existence is evil. Second, *transmigration*, with the doctrine of *karma*: all living beings are subject to an indefinite series of reincarnations, and the conditions of each incarnation are determined by the moral quality of acts performed in previous incarnations. Third, *salvation* lies in release from this chain of existences; it is to be gained primarily by *knowledge* of the supreme truth, which has a quasi-magic power of giving its possessor control over his destiny. As secondary or auxiliary means of salvation are mentioned morality, asceticism in some form or other, and devotion to a supreme being or prophetic personality. These seem originally to have been meant as aids to the attainment of saving knowledge, and they have little importance in the Upaniṣads; but in various later sects one or another of them at times becomes so important as to obscure the originally primary aim of "knowledge."

Chapter IV. *Prehistory of the God of the Bhagavad Gītā.* — The Deity of the Gītā seems to be a blend of the impersonal Upaniṣadic Absolute with a popular god or deified hero, Kṛṣṇa, who was identified with the Vedic god Viṣṇu. The combination thus formed contained, therefore, elements which could appeal to orthodox ritualists, to speculative intellectuals, and to the untutored masses.

SECOND PART: THE TEACHINGS OF THE BHAGAVAD GĪTĀ

Chapter V. *Soul and Body.* — All creatures are composed of two eternal and eternally distinct elements, soul and body. The body, including what are called "psychic" elements, is material; is subject to evolution, devolution, and change of all sorts; and consists of a blend of various elements or qualities. The soul is immaterial, uniform, unchangeable, without qualities, and inactive. All action is performed by the material body, upon other material bodies or substances. The soul neither acts nor is affected by action; indeed it is not affected by any influence outside of itself. It has only contemplative powers. Ordinary creatures, however, confuse body and soul, owing to the disturbing influence of the material organ of self-consciousness, and imagine that their souls act and suffer. The enlightened man realizes the true distinction between soul and body; his soul is thereby freed from the bondage of connection with the body, whence come action and suffering; and he attains release.

Chapter VI. *The Nature of God.* — God is pictured as the First Principle of the universe, the Soul of all; the highest or best part of all; the noblest aspect of all; immanent in all (sometimes even in what is considered evil, but sometimes only in what is considered good). God seems generally to be regarded as a principle distinct from either the soul or the body of individual beings, tho they are all "in Him." He transcends the universe. Sometimes the Upaniṣadic Brahman seems to be identified with God; but at other times Brahman is distinguished from God, and is then ordinarily subordinated to Him. At times God is spoken of dualistically; his "lower nature" is the empiric, material universe, his "higher nature" is supernal and beyond the ken of empiric creatures. God takes on individual incarnations to save the world of men; such an incarnation is Kṛṣṇa. His supreme form is revealed only as a rare act of grace to His elect; such an act of grace is granted to Arjuna, who beholds God's very Self in a mystic vision.

Chapter VII. *Action and Rebirth.*—Any action, good or bad, must normally have its effect in continued existence for the doer. But the Gītā says that this is due not to the action as such, but to *desire* underlying the action. Acts performed with indifference to the results, without interest in the outcome, have no binding effect. It is therefore unnecessary to renounce action altogether. It is even improper to do so — as well as impossible. We cannot refrain from action if we would, and we should not if we could. Man must do his duty, without desire or fear of the consequences. Most often duty is not defined; we are told simply to do our duty *qua* duty, as a sort of categorical imperative, without selfish interest. At other times attempts are made to define duty in terms of religious or social requirements, or on the basis of the oneness of man with his neighbors and with God, from which is deduced the duty of treating others as oneself.

Chapter VIII. *The Way of Knowledge and the Way of Disciplined Activity.* — The Gītā distinguishes two schools of thought which it calls Sāṃkhya and Yoga. By Sāṃkhya it means the doctrine of salvation thru the power of perfect knowledge, implying withdrawal from the world and renunciation of actions. By Yoga it means the opposing doctrine that one should seek emancipation by unselfish performance of duty. Both of these doctrines are recognized as leading to salvation, and in particular the power of knowledge is fully admitted in various places. Nevertheless the Gītā usually prefers the way of "indifference in action" or "disciplined activity," which is spoken of as leading to knowledge, or else as bringing salvation directly, and more "easily" than the way of knowledge and inaction.

Chapter IX. *The Way of Devotion to God.* — This is a still "easier" way of gaining salvation, and is most favored of all in the Gītā, altho it too is at times spoken of as bringing man to salvation indirectly, by perfecting him in "knowledge" or "discipline." By filling his being with love of God, and doing all acts as a service to God, man attains union with Him; that is, salvation. Sometimes God is spoken of as Himself intervening to help his devotees towards this goal. It is particularly important that man should fix his mind on God at the hour of death; this has a special tendency to bring the soul of the dying man to God.

Chapter X. *Attitude Towards Hindu Orthodoxy and Other Religious Be-*

liefs. — The Gītā contains some expressions that are distinctly hostile to the orthodox ritualistic religion. In general, however, it is tolerant of it, or even recommends the "disinterested" performance of its rites, as a matter of "duty." Towards rival religions in general its attitude is broad and tolerant; it admits a qualified validity to all acts of sincere religious devotion.

Chapter XI. *Practical Morality.* — While morality has only minor importance in the Gītā's scheme of salvation, immorality is usually regarded as a fatal obstacle to it. Desire is the most fundamental cause of vice. The most prominent specific ethical principle in the Gītā is that of doing good to others, treating others as oneself. Yet the injunction to do no harm to any living creature, tho it is a logical inference from that principle and tho it is very prominent in most Hindu ethical systems, is barely mentioned in the Gītā and receives no emphasis.

CHAPTER XIII

Conclusion

It has been my purpose in this book to let the Bhagavad Gītā tell its own story in the main, with as little comment of my own as possible. However, the mere topical arrangement of the Gītā's materials is in itself an implied comment; for it is wholly foreign to the Gītā itself, which constantly juxtaposes unrelated matters and widely separates passages dealing with the same subjects. And it has seemed to me, after all, neither desirable nor possible to refrain from indicating the relations between the various doctrines of the Gītā as they appear to me.

For this, to me, is what an interpretation must be. I should not know how to attempt any other kind. And I am obliged to believe that it is worth attempting; that if one succeeded, the result would help towards understanding the Gītā. To bring together its different answers to this or that question must surely be useful. And it does not prevent a true view of the book, so long as one is careful to emphasize the fact that logical arrangement is not intended in the book itself. This I have tried to make very clear. Without this proviso, it might perhaps be maintained that to present the book's doctrines in logical arrangement is to violate its spirit.

For, as we have now abundantly seen, the Gītā makes no attempt to be logical or systematic in its philosophy. It is frankly mystical and emotional. What we may, if we like, call its inconsistencies are not due to slovenliness in reasoning; nor do they express a balanced reserve of judgment. This is sufficiently proved in several cases by the fact that the Gītā deliberately brackets two opposing views and asserts the validity of both. It is only in the realm of logic that we must choose between yes and no, or else confess ignorance. The Gītā finds no difficulty in saying both yes and no, at the same time. For its point of view is simply unrelated to logic. Even what it calls "knowledge" is really intuitional perception; it is not, and is not intended to be, based on rational analysis. And, as we have seen, "knowledge" is not the Gītā's favorite "way of salvation." To the Gītā, as to the Christian mystics, reason is an uncertain and flickering light. The truly "wise" man should abandon it wholly and follow the "kindly Light," the *lux benigna*, of God's grace. He must sink his personality in ecstatic devotion to God, trusting absolutely in Him, and throwing upon Him all responsibility, doing all deeds as "acts of worship" to God. In the long run nothing else matters. Of course, the Gītā differs from the Christian mystics in some of its fundamental doctrines; for after all it is a Hindu work, and shares the common Hindu axioms. Yet in the practical outcome of its teachings it is astonishing to see how close it comes to many of them. It recalls them in its mystical, anti-rational point of view; in its ardent, personal, devotional theism; in its subjectivity, its focusing of the attention within, to the exclusion of all interest in that which is outside the individual's soul ("the Kingdom of God is within you"); and in its conception of the final goal as complete union with God, a state of supernal and indescribable bliss and peace.

There is one other characteristic of the Gītā's teachings, which seems to me to show such good psychology that it might be commended to the consideration of the Christian mystics; whether it is paralleled in their expressions or not, I do not know. The Gītā, we have seen, values the emotional and the concrete above the rational and the abstract *because* they are "easier." It is less troublesome to feel than to think. I take it that it needs no argument to prove the truth of this claim. It is equally evident that doctrines imbued with this spirit might naturally be expected to win popularity. I have already suggested that the enormous following which the Gītā has always had in India may be due in large part to its readiness to meet the ordinary man on his own ground, to make salvation as easy as possible for him. Objection might be raised against such an attitude from the rationalistic point of view; the rationalist may say that what is easier for man to grasp is not necessarily truer or as true. But from the Gītā's mystical point of view a man is as he feels; if he feels united with God, he is — or at least he shall be — united with God. And, speaking pragmatically, the Gītā's position is justified by the fact that many millions of men have found religious comfort in it, and expected salvation thru it. Who can say that they were disappointed? And if it should be granted that they were not, would not the Gītā have proved the usefulness of its doctrines, and so their pragmatic "truth"?

INDEX OF WORDS AND SUBJECTS

INDEX OF PASSAGES QUOTED OR REFERRED TO

CHAPTER 13

CHAPTER 14

CHAPTER 15

CHAPTER 16

CHAPTER 17

CHAPTER 18

71 72 73 12 11 10